THE PRACTICAL USE

OF THE

GREEK NEW TESTAMENT

THE PRACTICAL USE

OF THE

GREEK NEW TESTAMENT

by

KENNETH S. WUEST

Revised by

DONALD L. WISE

MOODY PRESS

CHICAGO

TO

That elect, and honorable, and enviable class of men that we call students of New Testament exegesis. Surely they are the happiest and the most enviable of all men, who have been set apart to nothing else but to the understanding and opening up of the hid treasures of God's Word and God's Son.[1]

1. Alexander Whyte in *The Walk, Conversation, and Character of Jesus Christ our Lord.*

PREFACE

It is one thing to have a theoretical knowledge of New Testament Greek. It is quite another to be able to use that knowledge in a practical way.

A Bible expositor may have an excellent training in the elements of Greek grammar and in syntax. He may know his declensions and conjugations perfectly. He may possess an extensive vocabulary, be well read in the Greek classics, and acquainted with the papyri. His library shelves may be stocked with the finest tools furnished by Greek scholarship. Yet with all that, it is possible that he may still have only a reading acquaintance with the Greek New Testament.

That man has just scratched the surface of the Greek text. He has never learned how to make a practical use of the rules of Greek grammar and syntax. He does not know how to dig down beneath the surface of the Greek New Testament, and uncover truth that the translations do not bring out. It is that untranslatable residue of truth that so enriches the life and ministry of the student of that Book of books.

The purpose of this volume is to demonstrate the method of using one's theoretical knowledge of New Testament Greek in a practical way. When the Bible expositor has acquired the knack of doing this, he has come into possession of the mystic secret of Greek exegesis.

Kenneth S. Wuest

Preface to the Revised Edition

Kenneth S. Wuest was one of those teachers whose influence went much further than the walls of his classroom. To him the classroom was more than merely an opportunity to convey some material. It was a commission from God to instruct, example, and motivate the student as well as explain and apply the meaning of the text of the Greek New Testament.

I have had the rare privilege of knowing him as my Greek professor, mentor, faculty colleague, and friend at Moody Bible Institute.

His unquestioned dedication to the inspiration and authority of the text of the Word of God and a spiritual life that literally permeated every class session were only exceeded by the enthusiasm with which he taught his classes. He firmly believed and practiced that enthusiasm is something that is caught, not taught.

A man who himself always displayed the fruit of the Spirit, he continually stressed the use of the Greek language in Bible study, but never for the purpose of parading it before one's listeners. His method of study and use of the material left his students with a desire to do the same in order to correctly understand and explain it so everyone could understand it. He often said, "Put the cookies on the bottom shelf where everyone can reach them."

This volume is the practical outgrowth of his belief that the intricate formation of the Greek language is God's tool to us in understanding the New Testament. Here he applies, as he did in the classroom, many of the basic elements and principles of the structure of the language as aids in interpreting the New Testament.

Donald L. Wise

Contents

CHAPTER   **PAGE**

1. The Practical Use of the Article   15
2. The Practical Use of Gender, Number,
   and Case   27
3. The Practical Use of Tense, Mood,
   and Voice   39
4. The Practical Use of Prepositions   57
5. The Practical Use of Synonyms   71
6. The Practical Use of Word Studies   83
7. The Practical Use of the Fuller or
   Expanded Translation   107
8. The Practical Method of Mastering the
   Greek Text in Preparation for Expository
   Preaching   115
9. The Practical Greek Student's Kit of Tools   127
10. The Practical Method of Presenting the
    Added Light from the Greek Text   135
11. The Practical Place of the Holy Spirit
    in the Interpretation of the Greek
    New Testament   143

1
The Practical Use of the Article

T<small>HE</small> definite article in Greek is the Greek index-finger pointing out individual identity. It frequently does more than that. It marks contrast. It makes the word with which it is used stand out distinctly. It points out an object and draws the reader's attention to it. The definite article in Greek was originally derived from the demonstrative pronoun, and it has retained some of the demonstrative force.

The Greek does not have an indefinite article comparable to the one in English. The absence of the definite article constitutes in Greek, where the context indicates, the equivalent of the indefinite article in English. The presence and the absence of the article must be carefully noted by the Greek student. *The presence of the article identifies. The absence of the article qualifies.* That is, when the article is used, the emphasis is upon particular identity, individuality, even uniqueness in some contexts, and upon contrast. When the article is not used, the emphasis is

15

upon the quality or character of the person or thing designated by the noun. The *articular*[1] noun identifies. The *anarthrous*[2] noun qualifies.

For instance, the Greek student, trained in the syntax of the definite article, when confronted with: Ἐν ἀρχῇ ἦν ὁ Λόγος, καὶ ὁ Λόγος ἦν πρὸς τὸν θεόν, καὶ θεὸς ἦν ὁ Λόγος (John 1:1), would react as follows: As for the absence of the article before ἀρχῇ, he would reason that since a prepositional phrase is qualitative in its character, the natural thing would be for the article to be left out, since that would be in accord with the genius of the prepositional phrase. In the translation he would offer, he would include the definite article, since the English reader would not understand the significance of its absence. Again, he would not offer the translation, "In a beginning was the Word," since he knows that the context is highly qualitative in its character and thus would not require an indefinite article in the translation. This is an *idiom in the Greek language*, which, of course, is impossible to handle in a translation.

But the presence of the article before λόγος points out particular identity. The Lord Jesus is not merely *a* concept of Deity, one among many. He is the particular, individual, unique concept of Deity. He is Deity told out. He is the only and the full concept of Deity. Coming to τὸν θεόν, the student would not translate "the God," for he knows that θεός used with the article refers to God the Father. As to θεός in its *anarthrous* use, he would not translate "the Word was a god," and for the reason that the context does not teach polytheism, and because the absence of the article here, qualifies. Therefore, the quality or character of Deity is emphasized. The translation would be, "The Word as to His essence was Deity."

Now, a student who has been trained only in the elements of Greek grammar, does not understand the significance of the presence or the absence of the Greek definite article. He needs a course in syntax. The pastor who has a reading acquaintance with the Greek New Testament that is based upon his study of the elements of Greek grammar, should pursue a study of syntax. *A Manual Grammar of the Greek New Testament*, by Dana and Mantey, is a book he can handle without a teacher. The material is clearly and simply presented. It is an intellectual delight to read and study it. The student of the Greek New Testament will find that he will be constantly referring to it for help in his solution of the problems of Greek exegesis.

A study of the use of the definite article will often solve a problem in exegesis that otherwise would remain unsolved. For instance, we have, "But before faith came, we were kept under the law, shut up unto the faith which should afterwards be revealed" (Gal. 3:23). As it stands in the English translation, the statement is made that faith came with the historic Christ. That would mean that faith was not exercised for salvation before the cross. But "Abraham believed God, and it was accounted to him for righteousness" (Gal. 3:6). We have a clear contradiction here in the English translation. The difficulty is solved by noting the presence of the article before the first occurrence of the word "faith" in 3:23. It is, "Before *the* faith came." One of the uses of the Greek article is to denote previous reference. For instance, the Samaritan woman asks our Lord, πόθεν οὖν ἔχεις τὸ ὕδωρ τὸ ζῶν; (John 4:11). The article is used with the words "water" and "living." Her question was, "From whence then do you have that water, that living water to which you just made reference?"

The article before the word "faith" identifies the faith spoken of in verse 23 with the previously mentioned faith in verse 22, personal faith in Jesus Christ as Savior, exercised in this age of grace. That faith is fundamentally alike in character to the faith exercised before the cross, but different in that it looks back to an accomplished salvation at the cross, whereas the faith exercised before the cross looked forward to the accomplishment of that salvation at Calvary. The former is faith in an *historic* Christ, the latter, faith in a *prophetic* Christ. Faith as such did not begin to be exercised at the cross. But the particular faith in Jesus Christ as exercised in this age of grace came in at the beginning of the age of grace. Thus, a rather difficult problem in exegesis is solved by the syntax of the article. The Greek student, puzzled by the English translation here, would note the *articular* use of the word "faith," consult Dana and Mantey on the Article, and find his difficulty resolved for him.

Take the difficulty found in the statement, "Though he were a Son, yet learned he obedience by the things which he suffered' (Heb. 5:8). The Christian is a son of God (Gal. 3:26 υἱός, son), and he learns obedience by the things which he suffers. There is no point in saying that in spite of the fact that the Lord Jesus was a Son of God, He learned obedience by His suffering. The word is *anarthrous* here. Quality and character are stressed. The indefinite article should not be in the translation. The idea is, "though He were Son in character, Very God of Very God, He learned obedience." God renders obedience to no one. There is no being higher than God whom He could obey. But in spite of the fact that the Lord Jesus is Son of God in character, thus, God the Son, He in His humanity learned obedience by the things which He suffered. He in His omniscience knew what obedience was before He became incarnate. But He came to know what obedience was *in experience* when He as the Man Christ Jesus, obeyed God the Father. *Thus, another difficulty is cleared up by the simple application of a rule of Greek syntax.*

Or, take the statement, "God is love" (1 John 4:8). *That simply is not true.* The rule of syntax in a case like this is that, when the article is used with the predicate, it shows the essential identity of the predicate with the subject. For instance, ἡ ἁμαρτία ἐστὶν ἡ ἀνομία (1 John 3:4), makes sin identical with lawlessness. They are of the same essence. But the expression, "God is love" is ὁ θεὸς ἀγάπη ἐστίν (1 John 4:8). The word in the predicate is *anarthrous*. That means that quality, character, or nature are stressed. The idea is "God as to His nature is love." The subject and the predicate are not in this case essentially identical. God is a person, infinite, eternal, omniscient, omnipresent, and omnipotent in His being. *He has a nature that is loving.* The same holds true with the statement, "God is a Spirit" (John 4:24). Angels and demons are called spirits in the New Testament. They are created intelligences. But that is not true of God. He is the Creator. What the Lord Jesus said to the woman was, "God as to His nature is spirit" (incorporeal being). Thus, He must be worshipped in the sphere of the human spirit and in the energy of the Holy Spirit.

The words in 1 Peter 3:1 present a difficulty; "Likewise, ye wives, be in subjection to your own husbands; that, if any obey not the word, they also may without the word be won by the conversation of the wives." Here is the case of some Christian wives attempting to win their stiff-necked, obstinate husbands to the Lord. The first mention of λόγος clearly refers to the Word of God. The definite article *in the translation* clearly refers the second use of λόγος to the Word of God. But how can those husbands be won to the Lord Jesus aside from or without the Word of God? The solution to the difficulty lies in the fact that whereas the first occurrence of λόγος is *articular,* the second use is *anarthrous.* The indefinite article should appear in the translation in conection with the second use of λόγος. That is, those Christian wives who have given their husbands the gospel over and over again, should stop speaking to them about their souls, lest they get to nagging, and more harm than good be done. They are to live Christlike lives before them now, and without *a word* from the wife, win the husbands to the Lord. Their husbands know the gospel story and how to be saved. The testimony of the Christian woman's life will be used of God to bring them to the place where they will put their faith in the Lord Jesus. *Again, a little attention paid to the Greek syntax of the article has cleared up an exegetical difficulty.*

I heard a pastor preach a funeral sermon in which he included the departed saint in the great multitude spoken of in Revelation 7:14, who "came out of great tribulation." The words "great tribulation" are of general application, referring to the tribulations, trials, and heartaches which all the saints experience. But a glance at the Greek text gives us ἐκ τῆς θλίψεως τῆς μεγάλης. θλίψεως is *articular*, speaking of a particular tribulation, and the adjective μεγάλης, also *articular*, identifies this particular tribulation as the great one. When the article is repeated with some word or phrase that modifies the noun, we have a construction that is used to give emphasis to the word that modifies that noun, and the article functions as a mild relative pronoun. Thus, the saints in the Revelation passage will be martyred and come out of "the tribulation which is the great one." The analysis of the Revelation further identifies that tribulation as the one which will occur after the rapture of the church. The speaker had the departed saint chronologically misplaced because he did not consult the Greek text and the syntax of the articles in the expression. *One simply cannot afford to neglect the Greek article if one wants to do accurate exegesis in the New Testament.* It is true that the Revised Version has included the definite article in its rendering of this expression. But the King James Version still remains the popular translation of the English-speaking world, and so it is necessary to call the student's attention to this matter of the study of the Greek article.

The Greek article will sometimes give the student the key to the understanding of an entire section of Scripture. For instance, does Romans 6 deal with the kind of a life the Christian should live or with the method of living that life? Does the word "sin" in, "Shall we continue in sin, that grace may abound?" (Rom. 6:1), refer to acts of sin or the evil nature? A glance at the Greek text will show that the word "sin" is preceded by the article. The article identifies the sin referred to as a particular kind defined by the context. It points to the sin spoken of in 5:21, and indicates that Paul is still speaking of the same sin. The sin in 5:21 is said to "reign as king." All of which means that the sin spoken of in Romans 6 is not an act but a nature. That means that this chapter deals with the *method* of living a Christian life, not with the kind of life one should live. It deals with the mechanics of the Spirit-filled life. *Thus, a little attention paid to the use of the Greek article has led the way to a correct exegesis of this entire section.*

Some would interpret the words, "A bishop must be . . . the husband of one wife," and, "Let the deacons be the husbands of one wife" (1 Tim. 3:2, 12), as requiring those church officials to be married, and thus barring unmarried men from those offices. But a glance at the Greek text will show that the words "husband" and "wife" are both *anarthrous.* That means that quality, or character, is stressed. It is the character of the bishop and the deacon that is in Paul's mind, and this agrees with the context, in which the personal qualities of those individuals are mentioned. It is not that they must be married, but that if they are married, they must be men of such a character that they will have only one wife. It is a prohibition of polygamy. They must be "one-wife sort of husbands." A delicate problem in church organization could be solved, should such arise in a local church, by means of the application of a simple rule of Greek syntax.

There is a rule in Greek syntax that is connected with the presence and absence of the article, called Granville Sharp's rule. It is as follows: "When the copulative καί connects two nouns of the same case, if the article ὁ or any of its cases precedes the first of the said nouns or participles, and is not repeated before the second noun or participle, the latter always relates to the same person that is expressed or described by the first noun or participle, denoting a further description of the first-named person."[3] In other words, when two nouns in the same case are connected by καί, and the first noun is *articular*, and the second is *anarthrous*, the second noun refers to the same person or thing to which the first noun refers, and is a further description of it.

This rule is of invaluable assistance to the exegete. For instance, the word "foreknowledge" occurs first in the New Testament, in Acts 2:23. Its usage here should throw a flood of light upon the usage of the word in other places where it is found. The word πρόγνωσις in classical Greek meant merely previous knowledge. But here it means more than that, as our rule of syntax brings out. The words, "Him, being delivered by the determinate counsel and foreknowledge of God," are in the Greek text τοῦτον τῇ ὡρισμένῃ βουλῇ καὶ προγνώσει τοῦ θεοῦ. βουλῇ is *articular*, προγνώσει *anarthrous*. The latter word refers to the same act that the former refers to. That will give us our clue to the New Testament usage of πρόγνωσις when it is used in connection with God. βουλῇ refers to the counsel that is the result of the deliberations of a council; here, a council composed of the three members of the triune God. The participle describing βουλῇ is perfect in tense, indicating that the deliberations of the council had been concluded and the members had come to a decision. The verb ὁρίζω means "to fix limits upon, to mark out the boundaries of, to determine, appoint." Thus, the purpose of the council was to appoint the member of the triune God who would become the Lamb to be slain. πρόγνωσις in classical Greek, we noted, meant merely "foreknowledge." But here it partakes of the nature of the meaning of the noun *with which it is grammatically connected*, βουλῇ, and is a further description of it. The βουλή was one in which the Lord Jesus was appointed to a certain destiny. That act is also referred to by the word προγνώσει, which by this association has added to itself in the New Testament, the idea of foreordination, where it is used in connection with an act of God. *Thus, a rule of Greek syntax has opened up to us the New Testament content of meaning of this word.*

The wording in 2 Peter 1:1, "the righteousness of God and our Saviour Jesus Christ," might lead some who are not acquainted with the theology of the New Testament to conclude that there are two persons mentioned and that the Savior is not God. But the construction in the Greek text conforms to Granville Sharp's rule. The words, "Saviour Jesus Christ," refer to the same person that the word "God" refers to. Thus, the rules of Greek syntax require us to understand that the Lord Jesus Christ is God. The translation reads, "Our God and Saviour Jesus Christ," the pronoun "our" referring to both "God" and "Saviour" since both designations refer to the same Person.

We will look at one more instance in which this rule of Greek syntax brings to light precious truth that would possibly be overlooked. In Ephesians 4:11, the words 'pastors" and "teachers" are in the construction with which we have been dealing. We are' required to understand, therefore, that the two designations refer to the same individual. That means that every man whom God calls to be a pastor, has, in addition to his pastoral gift, also been given a teaching gift. It is for him to develop that gift. That means, again, that the pastor after God's own heart is one who exercises a didactic ministry. Thus, we have two important facts that every pastor should know, and that do not appear in the English translation, but are brought out by the simple application of a rule of Greek syntax.

There is a use of the article entirely lost in an English translation, and for the reason that it is an idiom peculiar to the Greek language. It is the use of the article with adverbs and clauses. In Philippians 1:3-5, Paul thanks God for the fellowship of the Philippians from the first day (when Lydia opened her home to the preaching of the gospel) until τοῦ νῦν. The word "now" does not mark only a point in time here, but a point in time particularized by the gift which the Philippians had sent. The article before the word "now" marks it out as distinct in its identity. That which gives that point of time distinctness from other points of time is the generosity of the Philippian saints.

In Mark 9:22, the father of the child said to Jesus, "If thou canst do anything, have compassion on us, and help us." Jesus said, "If thou canst." The word "believe" is not in the best texts. The article is used with the phrase "if thou canst." It is an index-finger, pointing out that phrase and holding it up for particular attention. That article is full of meaning. Jesus was warning the man against a lack of faith implied in the expression, "If thou canst."

The foregoing presentation of the practical use of the rules of Greek syntax in relation to the article is not exhaustive but merely illustrative and has, we trust, demonstrated the value of using one's Greek New Testament in the exegesis of the Word of God. The student who has had only the elements of Greek should purchase a copy of *A Manual Grammar of the Greek New Testament*, by Dana and Mantey, and make himself proficient in its rules of syntax. The book is ably written. Its contents are simply and clearly presented. One does not need a teacher to help one master this book.

1. The noun preceded by the article.
2. The noun not preceded by the article.
3. *A Manual Grammar of the Greek New Testament* by Dana and Mantey (MacMillan Company, NY), p. 147.

2
The Practical Use of Gender, Number and Case

G ENDER, number, and case can be used in a practical way. For instance, in Romans 6:12, does the word "it" refer to "sin" or to "body"? Does Paul have reference to obedience to the lusts (desires) of sin or to those of the body? One could argue that the pronoun referred to "sin," since "sin" is desirous of reigning, and the exhortation is against obeying certain desires defined in the context. In other words, the ideas of reigning and obeying are closely allied, and therefore the word "it" refers back to "sin." The argument is most plausible. *But this interpretation is exploded by the simple application of the rule of Greek syntax which says that the pronoun agrees with its antecedent in gender and number.* The word "sin" is feminine, the word "body" neuter, and the word "it" neuter. All of which means that it is the lusts of the body concerning which Paul is speaking. This is final. It ends all further discussion. A rule of Greek grammar like this is just as sure as the mathematical rule that two and two make four.

The man who knows his Greek is therefore, all other things being equal, the more accurate expositor of the Word, and is less apt to make mistakes in interpretation.

Someone who does not accept the doctrine of the virgin birth of the Lord Jesus, could argue that the pronoun "whom" in Matthew 1:16 referred to Joseph and Mary. But a glance at the Greek text gives us ἧς, the feminine singular relative pronoun. The antecedent of this pronoun must be feminine in gender and singular in number. It is obvious that the pronoun "whom" could not refer to both Joseph and Mary, for in that case it would be plural in number. It could not refer to the name Joseph, since the latter is given in the lexicon as masculine in gender. It must refer only to the name Mary, since the latter is both singular in number and feminine in gender. Thus, the simple application of a rule of Greek grammar can be used to support a cardinal doctrine of Christianity and clarify an issue with which one may be confronted. I remember well the effect this demonstration had upon an individual who wanted more light on this matter. He could see that his answer, based upon the rules of Greek grammar, was accepted as conclusive and final.

Take the translation of 1 Peter 1:7, "That the trial of your faith, being much more precious than of gold that perisheth, though it be tried with fire, might be found unto praise and honor and glory at the appearing of Jesus Christ."

Is it the trial or the faith that is more precious? Is it more precious than the trial of gold or more precious than gold? Is it the faith or the gold which is tried by fire? A glance at the Greek text discloses the fact that the word "trial" is nominative case, neuter gender. The verb of being is understood. This verb is followed by the predicate nominative. The words, "much more precious," are the translation of a neuter singular comparative adjective in the nominative case. That means that Peter is teaching here that the trial, not the faith, is more precious. Furthermore, Peter is not teaching here that the approved faith is more precious. The assayer's report to the mining company is of far more value than the gold he has assayed. The fact that a certain Christian has been put to the test and has met that test, and thus has demonstrated that he can be trusted by God, is of far more value to God than his approved faith. God has someone He knows He can trust.

Is the trial of faith more precious than the trial of gold or than gold itself? A careful student of the English translation would say that in view of the preposition "of," the trial of faith is more precious than the trial of gold. Yet a knowledge of the Greek here helps to make things clearer. The word "gold" is in either of two cases in the Greek, the genitive or the ablative. It could be the ablative of comparison, in which construction the word in the ablative case is the standard of comparison in the comparative clause. Or, it could be the genitive of description. In that case, the demonstrative pronoun in the neuter gender and the ablative case would be understood, and would be the standard of comparison. The translation would read "than that of gold." The context will have to decide. Since it is the trial that is more precious, it must be the trial of faith that is more precious than the trial of gold, the two trials being compared.

Then, the question comes up, does the pronoun "it" refer to the faith that is tried by fire, or does it have reference to the gold? *The problem is quickly solved by the Greek text.* The words, "though it be tried," are the translation of a concessive participle, neuter in gender, genitive in case, referring not to "faith" which is feminine, but to "gold" which is neuter. Thus, the expanded translation reads: "that the approval (δοκίμιον) of your faith, that faith having been put to the test for the purpose of being approved, that approval being much more precious than the approval of gold which perishes, though that gold is approved through fire-testing." The Bible expositor now can really come to grips with this verse. The first step in attempting to explain the meaning of a portion of Scripture to someone else is that of coming to understand it clearly yourself. When the saint in the pew asks the question, "Just what is the preacher driving at?" it is because the preacher himself does not have a clear understanding of the portion he is expounding. Clear Bible exposition is based upon a clear apprehension of the Word by the expositor. And the latter is acquired by good hard work, the tools furnished by scholarship, and a dependence upon the Holy Spirit.

Take the problem presented in the translation of Matthew 3:11: "I indeed baptize you with water . . . he shall baptize you with the Holy Ghost." Are we to understand from these statements that, just as water was applied to the believer by John, so the Holy Spirit is applied to the believer by the Lord Jesus? That is, does the baptism that is connected with the Spirit, result in the coming of the Spirit to take up His residence in the believer? The expressions in the English translation and also in the Greek text are alike. Both use the same prepositions.

The way the expositor trained in Greek syntax would go about solving this problem is as follows: the preposition ἐν is followed by either one of two cases, the locative or the instrumental. He would consult Dana and Mantey on the various classifications of these two cases. The classifications of these cases depend upon and are an outgrowth of the context in which the word in either one of these cases is found. John said literally, "I baptize you in water." There is a use of the locative called "the locative of place." An example would be, "The disciples came in the little boat"

(John 21:8). The locative case here imposes limits. These limits are the gunwales of the boat. The coming of the disciples was within the limits of a boat. These limits are called spatial. John baptized his converts in the Jordan River. The limits of his action of baptizing them were the banks of the Jordan. These were spatial limits. Thus we have the locative of place.

Now we come to the statement, "He shall baptize you with the Holy Ghost." The locative of place will not do here. The Holy Ghost is not a place that imposes spatial limitations upon the act of baptizing. Therefore, the Holy Spirit is not in this baptism placed in the believer as John applied water to his converts.

We look for a classification that will fit the context in which the word "baptize" is used in this statement. There is the statement, "Blessed are the pure in heart" (Matt. 5:8). Here limitations are placed upon those who are pure. Those whose purity is in the sphere of the heart are blessed. In the background of our Lord's thinking here were the Jewish ritualists of the day who claimed to be pure. But their purity was merely an outward one, a purity which was the result of ceremonial observances. Our Lord speaks of those who are pure actually, and inwardly. Here we have limitations imposed by the character of the purity referred to. These are not spatial but logical. We have here, therefore, the locative of sphere. The translation could read, "Blessed are those who are pure in the sphere of the heart."

Thus, the statement of John, "He shall baptize you with the Holy Ghost," could also read, "He shall baptize you in the sphere of the Holy Ghost." The locative of sphere is defined by Dana and Mantey[1] as follows: "It is the confining of one idea within the bounds of another, thus indicating the sphere within which the former idea is to be applied." Thus, the baptism which is associated with our Lord is one that has to do with the Spirit, not with water. While the locative of sphere does not define for us the relationship the Spirit sustains to this baptism, yet it does make clear that the Holy Spirit is not placed in the believer in the baptism that is associated with Him, as water is applied to the believer in the case of John's baptism. We have been saved from an error which is taught in some branches of the visible church; namely, that in the baptism that is associated with the Spirit, the Spirit comes to take up His residence in the believer to give him power for holy living and for service.

For light on the meaning of Spirit-baptism, we turn to 1 Corinthians 12:13 where we have, "For through the personal agency of one Spirit we all were baptized (placed) into one body." Thus, the purpose of the baptism by the Spirit is to unite the believing sinner to the Lord Jesus as his living Head (Rom. 6:3-4), and to place him into the mystical Body of Christ of which He is the Head (1 Cor. 12:13). Thus, an important point in doctrine is made clear, which has to do with the believer's relationship to the Holy Spirit, and which plays a vital part in his life.

An examination of the Greek text of Jude 6-7, would save the expositor from a rather bad blunder due to a misplaced comma in the King James Version. A comma in the wrong place can sometimes cover up some facts that are clearly taught in the Greek New Testament. In verse 6, the statement is made that the angels which sinned are reserved for judgment. In verse 7 we are informed that Sodom, Gomorrah, and the cities around them were judged. The words, "even as," connecting those two principal statements, show that the angels and the cities mentioned are alike in the sense that both are judged for their sins. The sin of the inhabitants of those cities is designated as fornication. Verse 6 does not specify the particular kind of sin of which the angels were guilty.

The commas after "Gomorrah" and "manner" lead the expositor to conclude that the meaning of verse 7 is as follows: *Sodom and Gomorrah, who gave themselves over to fornication and went after strange flesh, and the cities about them in like manner to Sodom and Gomorrah who did the same, are set forth for an example, suffering the vengeance of eternal fire.* This punctuation associates the phrase "in like manner" grammatically with the phrase "the cities about them," confining the sin of fornication to the cities mentioned in verse 7. The phrase "in like manner" is, however, an adverbial one, and the rules of *English* grammar demand that it be associated, not with the noun "cities," but with the verbal forms "giving themselves over to fornication" and "going after strange flesh." The rules of *Greek* grammar do the same.

In the Greek text the words, "Sodom and Gomorrah" and "the cities," are in the nominative case. The words, "giving themselves over to fornication" and "going after," are aorist participles in the nominative plural in apposition with the words "Sodom," "Gomorrah," and "the cities." The phrase "in like manner" is in the accusative case, and because it speaks of manner, is classified as an adverbial accusative. Dana and Mantey[2] say that "It (the accusative case) certainly belongs in a particular way to the verb." They give an illustration of the adverbial accusative of manner in the sentence δωρεὰν ἐλάβετε, δωρεὰν δότε (Matt. 10:8), where the words in the accusative case indicate *how* the action of the verb is to be performed.

The words, "in like manner," are associated grammatically, not with the words "Sodom" and "Gomorrah" and "the cities," which are in the nominative case, but with the two verbal forms, the participles "giving themselves over to fornication" and "going ·after strange flesh." A word in the accusative case in Greek is not associated grammatically with the word in the nominative case, but with the verb. Thus, the punctuation, based upon the rules of Greek syntax, should be, "Even as Sodom and Gomorrah and the cities about them, in like manner giving themselves over to fornication and going after strange flesh, are set forth for an example, suffering the vengeance of eternal fire." This is the punctuation offered by both the Eberhard and the Irwin Nestle Greek texts, and the text of Westcott and Hort. The Greek words are verbally inspired, and that inspiration extends to the grammar and syntax associated with the words, for the Holy Spirit led the writers to use the language spoken by the people who would read the Greek manuscripts of the New Testament. The correct understanding of the sentences is dependent upon the grammatical and syntactical constructions used. Those textual critics punctuated their texts on the basis of the rules of Greek grammar and syntax. Although we do not claim inspiration and infallibility for this punctuation, yet in view of the well-known and acknowledged rules of Greek syntax referred to above, we would say that, in the case at hand, the punctuation of the textual critics is correct.

Now, to what do the words, "in like manner," refer? The text, punctuated as we have just indicated, would refer the words to the angels of verse 6. That is, Sodom and Gomorrah and the cities about them, in like manner to the angels, committed fornication. And that is correct. But the Greek text gives us further help. The demonstrative pronoun τούτοις appears immediately after the words "in like manner." The King James Version takes no note of it, but the Revised Version translates the word. That is, those cities gave themselves over to fornication in like manner to these, namely, the angels. Thus we have a clear statement in the Greek text that angels committed fornication and went after strange flesh. *One such statement in the Word of God is enough to establish the fact.*

It will not do to attempt to break the force of the statement by saying that the fornication on the part of the angels was spiritual, not physical, for σάρξ means *corporeal being*. The word "strange" is the translation of ἕτερος. The angels transgressed the limits of their own natures to invade the realm of created beings of a different nature. It will not do to reject the plain statement of the Greek text by saying that the angels cannot commit fornication, and therefore they did not. *One does not measure what he is to believe in the Bible by what accords with his reason. That is pure and simple modernism.* The fact is that the Greek New Testament clearly states that angels committed fornication. This understanding of the statements in Jude is based upon the application of the rules of Greek syntax, in this case, rules so universally held that no Greek scholar would quarrel with them. So often, the mistake is made of interpreting the English Bible without any reference to or dependence upon the rules of English grammar. We know the English language. It is our mother tongue. We have forgotten, if we ever knew, the rules of English grammar, and hence bring our every day use of the English language to the task of interpreting the Word, faulty as that usage may be,—a most unscientific procedure. One will have to accept the fact of the angels committing fornication, repugnant and unexplainable as it is, or reject the verbal inspiration of the New Testament and the rules of Greek syntax. Thus, the simple application of the rules of Greek syntax has brought out a fact recorded in the Greek New Testament, which was covered up by faulty punctuation in the King James Version.

Let us look at an instance where the number of a word will throw light upon the English translation. The Lord Jesus said to Nicodemus, "Marvel not that I said unto thee, Ye must be born again" (John 3:7). Although the King James Version distinguishes between the singular and the plural of the personal pronoun here, we submit that the average reader of the English Bible does not. Such things are not often noticed because the student of the English Bible does not study the Bible with the rules of English grammar in mind. Nor does he use those rules in arriving at his interpretation. Herein lies one of the values of a knowledge of the Greek New Testament. Greek is a new and a difficult language to the student. In order to learn it, he must learn his grammar and syntax, his declensions and conjugations. These are part of his mental processes when he uses his Greek New Testament. Thus a σοί and a ὑμᾶς are more than a "thee" and a "ye" to him. The student of the English Bible ought to react to the "thee" and the "ye" by saying that the "thee" is the singular of the pronoun of the second person and the "ye," the plural of the pronoun of the second person. But he usually does not. A Greek student, on the other hand, has a mental picture of the declension, σύ σοῦ σοί σέ, and at once identifies σοί as the dative singular of the pronoun of the second person, and ὑμᾶς as the accusative plural of the same pronoun. Then he asks himself the question, "Why did the Lord Jesus change from the singular to the plural pronoun?" Here is a single inquirer seeking the way of salvation. Why did not Jesus use σέ? The answer is that Jesus in using ὑμᾶς, referred, not only to Nicodemus, but to his associates in the Sanhedrin. And the reason He did that is because He recognized the fact that Nicodemus was the representative of and was speaking for the San-hedrin. This our Lord surmised by Nicodemus's use of the first person plural οἴδαμεν. The latter was giving Jesus the

consensus of opinion then prevalent among the members
of this Jewish council. Jesus, by the use of the plural
number of the pronoun, sent His message back to this
august body through Nicodemus. It was not only Nicodemus, but all of his associates as well, that needed to be
born again. Thus, a little attention paid to the number of
a word, will bring out a point which an English reader
would often overlook. All of which means that the expositor who knows and uses his Greek will be more accurate in
his interpretation, and will present richer, more detailed,
and deeper truth than the one who has access only to a
translation.

This kind of work makes for the accurate exegete. The
surgeon who keeps his instruments well sharpened always
does better work than the one who does not. The Bible
expositor who brings to his study of the New Testament a
keen appreciation and understanding of the tools of Greek
scholarship will always do better work than the one who
does not use them. The Holy Spirit can better use a man
who has a clear understanding of the Word and presents it
in a clearer and simpler way than He can the man who
does not have such a keen, deep insight into its meaning.
The Word is the tool the Spirit uses. The sharper the tool,
the better work He can do in the hearts of those who
listen. After all, it is not the preacher who does the work.
His responsibility is to put into the hands of the Holy
Spirit a clear, accurate Bible exposition which He can use
in the hearts of the people. Other professions dealing with
far less important departments of a person's life demand
the highest type of thoroughly trained experts. And yet,
somehow, the rank and file of those who minister the
Word are content to do the best they can without personally
using the tools of scholarship. They have half a dozen
translations, shelves of commentaries and other helps, and
this is as it should be. But all this does not take the place

of a personal, first-hand knowledge of the Greek New Testament. It is not required that a preacher be a Greek scholar. He cannot be both a good pastor and an excellent Greek scholar at the same time. He does not have time nor energy to be an expert in both lines of activity. But he can make himself acquainted with Greek grammar and syntax, use Greek word studies, and in that way obtain at first hand much rich truth, fresh with the dew of heaven upon it. The preacher's audience soon comes to recognize second hand truth which has the musty odor of ancient volumes about it. The people sense the fact when the pastor is just repeating truth he picked up here and there and somehow got together into a sermon. But when the pastor comes to his pulpit fresh from a session with his Greek New Testament, the truth falls on the ears of the waiting people as manna fell upon the Israelites. They will feast on wafers made with the honey that still drips from the comb. *And that comb is the Greek New Testament.*

I have always had a great admiration for that great New Testament Greek scholar, Dr. A. T. Robertson. I confess to the habit of living at times in his biography, just for the purpose of rubbing elbows, so to speak, with a man of such vast scholarship, and of gathering inspiration from his life so filled with prodigious labors in the field of the Greek New Testament.

Two sentences in this biography stand out for me. The biographer, referring to Dr. Robertson says: "As his knowledge of the grammar of the Greek of the New Testament grew, the accuracy of his exposition thereby was increased. The grammarian and the expositor thus walked side by side."[3]

1. *Manual Grammar of the Greek New Testament*, p. 87.
2. *Manual Grammar of the Greek New Testament*, pp. 91, 93.
3. *A. T. Robertson, A Biography*, Everett Gill (MacMillan Company, NY, 1943), p. 108.

3

The Practical Use of Tense, Mood, and Voice

THE SIMPLE application of the rules of Greek grammar and syntax will often lead one to the discovery of some tremendous truth which would be passed by unnoticed in the use of the English translation, or even of the Greek text when the rule is not deliberately called to mind and applied to the exegetical problem under consideration.

For instance, in Galatians 4:19 we have, "My little children, of whom I travail in birth again until Christ be formed in you." The phrase under consideration is, "Christ be formed in you." "Be formed" is from μορφόομαι, a Greek philosophical term referring to the outward expression one gives of his inmost being, an expression which comes from and is representative of one's inner being. We could translate, "Christ be outwardly expressed in you." The verb is unmistakably passive in voice, since it is aorist in tense, the middle and passive voices in this tense appearing in different forms. We are on absolutely sure ground here and can bear down on the full significance of the passive voice in our interpretation. The definition of the passive voice is in two parts: *first*, the subject of the verb is inactive, passive, and *second*, it is acted upon by someone or something else.

We will apply the first part of our definition. The tremendous truth brought out is that the Lord Jesus, resident in the heart of the believer, lives there in an inactive or passive state. But that inactivity or passivity is defined and limited by the meaning of the verb. Surely, He is not inactive when it comes to fellowshipping with the saint or ministering in behalf of the saint in His office as advocate. But He is inactive and passive so far as expressing Himself in and through the life of the saint is concerned. That is the truth brought out. The Lord Jesus does not express Himself through the saint. He does not glorify Himself in the life of the Christian.

The other part of the definition gives us the truth that He is acted upon by someone else, and for the purpose of expressing Him and His beauty in and through the life of the saint. That person who acts upon the Lord Jesus and expresses Him through the life of the saint is the Holy Spirit. Paul devotes chapter 5 of Galatians to that very subject. Our Lord in John 16:14, speaking of the Holy Spirit, said ἐκεῖνος ἐμὲ δοξάσει. The pronoun of the remote person is used. The idea is, *"I* will not glorify Myself, but *that One* (the Holy Spirit), will glorify Me." *And that is the second of the tremendous truths brought out by the simple application of the rules of grammar.*

The practical lesson one gets from this is that if the Lord Jesus is to be seen in the life of the saint, it must be through the ministry of the Holy Spirit, and that ministry is performed only to the extent that the saint lives a yielded life in dependence upon Him.

Again, the simple application of a rule of syntax will sometimes settle a matter that has been debated for a long time, and settle it once and for all, unless one wishes to close his eyes to Greek grammar and syntax. Take the question of whether Paul wrote the entire letter to the Galatians in Greek uncials, or only the concluding portion, 6:11-18.

One expositor says that the words, "I have written," mark the point at which Paul takes up the pen into his own hand, and that the boldness of the handwriting answers to the force of the apostle's convictions. Of seven expositors whom I consulted on this passage in preparation for *Galatians in the Greek New Testament,* only one says that Paul wrote the entire epistle in Greek uncials. The others think that he wrote only the concluding remarks, and in inch-high capital letters to emphasize the conclusion.

The King James Version gives us, "Ye see how large a letter I have written unto you with my own hand." But the instrumental case and plural number of πηλίκοις γράμμασιν require us to translate, "Ye see with what large letters I wrote to you with my own hand."

ἔγραψα is aorist indicative, which combination of tense and mood refers to an event that took place in past time. If ἔγραψα refers to the conclusion of the letter only, how are we to understand this, since the writing of the conclusion was yet a future event to the apostle when he wrote this sentence? If Paul had referred to the conclusion of the letter he was about to write, he would have used the present tense as he does in 2 Thessalonians 3:17. The writing of the previous portion of the letter was a past event with Paul as he was writing this sentence. This means that Paul is stating the fact that he wrote that portion of the letter with his own hand in uncial Greek letters. He would not, therefore, be referring to the concluding portion of the letter. This interpretation is based upon the normal use of the aorist indicative.

But as we consult Dana and Mantey on the varied uses of the aorist tense, we find a classification called *The Epistolary Aorist*. That is listed by these scholars under the *Special Uses of the Aorist* and is based upon a knowledge of a custom observed by a Greek writer of a letter in the first century. The writer would sometimes place himself at the viewpoint of his reader and look at his letter as the recipient would do when he received it, namely, as a past event, whereas the actual writing of the letter was a present event with him. It was a courtesy extended to the reader of the letter. The point is that when the writer uses *the epistolary aorist*, he is looking at his *entire* letter, that which he has already written and that which he is about to write, as a past event, and for the reason that he has put himself at the viewpoint of the reader who will look at the *entire* letter as a past event. Thus, a simple rule of Greek syntax solves a problem which may have plausible arguments on both sides, but which arguments may not be final, since they are not based upon historical background and Greek syntax.

The uses of the present and aorist tenses are clearly defined in the potential moods. For instance, the *present imperative* with μή demands the cessation of an action that is already in progress, whereas the aorist subjunctive in a prohibition is an exhortation against doing a thing not yet begun. This distinction between these tenses in the potential moods was discovered, Moulton, the great Greek scholar tells us, by his friend Davidson who heard a Greek command his dog to stop barking by using μή with the present imperative.

The application of this rule of syntax, in the case of the present imperative expressed in a prohibition, throws a flood of light upon the kind of lives the recipients of the Pauline epistles were living. For instance, Paul wrote the

Philippians, "Stop perpetually worrying about even one thing" (Phil. 4:6). The point is, they were worrying. He wrote the Ephesian saints, "Stop having constant fellowship with the works of darkness" (5:11). There was a tendency among the saints there to keep up with the old associations. Some of them had not made a complete break with the world. He wrote to the Roman Christians, "Stop perpetually assuming an outward expression, an expression that does not come from within your innermost beings but is assumed from the outside, an expression patterned after this age" (Rom. 12:2). The fact is that the saints in the local church at Rome were still looking like the world out of which they were delivered by the blood of Christ.

An illustration of the use of the aorist subjunctive, exhorting against doing a thing not yet begun, is found in John 3:7, "Do not begin to marvel." Nicodemus was showing signs of doing so, and the Lord Jesus was anticipating him.

Excellent material for an evangelistic sermon is found in the use of the present participle and the aorist subjunctive in John 4:13-14, where our Lord says, "Whosoever *keeps on drinking* of this water shall thirst again. But whosoever *takes a drink* of the water that I shall give him shall never thirst." Continual drinking at the wells of the world never quenches the soul's thirst for heart satisfaction. But one drink of eternal life satisfies forever. The usual *aktionsart*[1] of the present tense in the indicative mood and in participles is durative action. The aorist subjunctive is punctiliar, speaking of the fact of the action. Here we have the mechanics of Greek syntax which produced the translation offered above. The reason why one drink of eternal life satisfies without a repeated drinking of the same, is given us in the context by the two words translated "well," φρεάρ and πηγή, the former speaking of a well into which water seeps, and which becomes stagnant and brackish; the latter referring to a spring, always fresh, overflowing, alive. The one drink of eternal life the believing sinner takes at the moment he is saved is in itself a supernatural spring, always alive, refreshing and satisfying the person in whom it has been placed by the power of God. Fresh touches like these, details so seldom heard in an evangelistic message because so few know Greek, and so few who do have access to the Greek New Testament ever use it, give that message a freshness and an originality that is welcomed by the saints in the audience, and make the message all the more usable in the hands of the Holy Spirit as He seeks to bring the lost to a saving knowledge of the Lord Jesus. But the point is, one must know his rules of syntax to be able to handle the Greek text in this way. And that means hard work.

Or, take the difficulty in 1 John 3:9 where the King James Version translates, "Whosoever is born of God doth not commit sin." That simply is not true. Christians do sin. The prohibitions in the Pauline epistles given in the present imperative with μή are enough to prove that Christians do sin, and this is corroborated by the Christian's own experience. We have in 1 John 2:15, "Stop constantly loving the world." The problem is solved when we note that the verb is in the present indicative, which the Greeks used for two purposes so far as *aktionsart* is concerned. They always used it to refer to durative action except where the context required punctiliar action. The context here states the fact that the Christian does sin. Therefore, punctiliar action cannot be used here. Both a wider and an immediate context require that we translate: "Whosoever is born of God, does not habitually sin." That is, John does not deny the fact that Christians sin. He does deny that they sin habitually as they did before they were saved.

In strict harmony with his position here, he uses the aorist subjunctive in 1 John 2:1 where he says, "In order that you may not commit an act of sin." He does not speak of the practice of sin, for that is not necessary, but of the commission of an act of sin. The *aktionsart* is punctiliar, not durative.

The person who asked Paul the questions in Romans 6:1 and 6:15 distinguished between the practice of sin in the Christian life and the committing of single acts of sin. The first question is in the present subjunctive, "Shall we continue to persist habitually in sin?" The second is in the aorist subjunctive, "Shall we commit an act of sin?" Paul's listener did not understand grace. He asked first whether the Christian should continue habitually to sustain the same relationship to the sinful nature that he sustained before he was saved. When told in Romans 6:2-14 that that was a mechanical impossibility since the power of sin was broken in the Christian's life and the divine nature implanted, he asks as to whether the Christian then is allowed to commit single acts of sin once in awhile. Paul's answer to the second question is that the Christian has changed masters, from Satan to Christ, and whereas while in the control of the evil nature he habitually served Satan, now in the control of the divine nature he habitually serves Christ. He has a nature now that makes him hate sin and love holiness.

Or, take the question as to whether Peter intended to throw his net into the sea for a brief fling at fishing again just until the Lord Jesus would come, or whether he purposed to go back to his fishing business permanently. John reports his words in Greek, ὑπάγω ἁλιεύειν (John 21:3). The infinitive is present in tense. In the infinitive, as well as in the potential moods, the *aktionsart* of the present and aorist tenses is clearly defined. The present is durative, the aorist punctiliar. Since the present tense loses its time implications when used with the infinitive and the potential moods, because the latter are both relatively future in their implications, and because the aorist is timeless, it is easy for the Greek to choose between them without being hampered by time restrictions. For instance, πιστεῦσαι means "to exercise faith on a certain occasion," while πιστεύειν means "to keep on constantly exercising faith," also "to be a believer." δουλεῦσαι means "to render an act of service," while δουλεύειν means "to serve continually," also, "to be a slave." Thus, ἁλιεύειν means "to keep on continually fishing," also "to be a fisherman." Thus, Peter was announcing to his fellow disciples that he was going back to his fishing business permanently. He was deserting his high calling of preaching the gospel to go back into the business from which the Lord had called him. The use of ὑπάγω shows that the function of the present infinitive as the writer has presented it, and the application of the implications of that function to the decision of Peter, are correct. ὑπάγω refers to a departure that involves a severing of one's antecedent relations. Peter was severing his connections with the Lord Jesus and his fellow-disciples so far as the preaching of the gospel was concerned. An examination of the rest of this chapter will indicate the harmony which exists between its contents and the interpretation offered above. Thus, a simple application of the rules of Greek grammar, settles a question that otherwise would continue to be debated with plausible arguments on both sides. The point is, however, that one simply must know his grammar to be able to use the Greek New Testament in a practical way.

The perfect tense in Greek is most illuminating, and casts a flood of light upon the interpretation of the Word. Take for instance, the contradiction between Paul's statements in Philippians 3:12 and 3:15. In 3:12, Paul denies

the fact that he is yet perfect (spiritually mature τέλειος).
In 3:15, he includes himself among those who are spiritually mature. The problem is solved by the simple application of the definition of the perfect tense. This tense
refers to an action which has been completed in past time,
this completed action having present results. Paul uses
τετελείωμαι, the perfect middle and passive. Since he
taught that a saint was brought to spiritual maturity, not
by his own efforts, but through the ministry of the Holy
Spirit, he had the passive voice in mind here, not the
middle. Thus, he denies the fact that he has been brought
by the Holy Spirit to the place in his Christian life where
the sanctifying work of the Holy Spirit is complete, beyond
which there would be no room for growth, and at which he
would stay in a position of absolute spiritual maturity that
would remain unchanged for the rest of his earthly life. In
3:15, he uses the adjective τέλειος. The verb of being is not
in the text, but is understood. Here he is speaking of
spiritual maturity, not in an absolute but in a relative sense.
The contradiction disappears when one understands that in
3:12 Paul denies the fact that he is spiritually mature in an
absolute sense, and in 3:15 asserts that he is spiritually
mature in a relative sense. Thus, the simple application of
the rules of Greek grammar here, has solved another
problem, and has given the exegete a correct understanding
of the passage in question.

Take our Lord's words in Matthew 4:4, "It is written."
Matthew reports them in one word γέγραπται. The full
translation of this verb in the perfect tense is, "It has been
written and as a result is at present on record." See the
truth now which comes from the application of this rule
of grammar. *First,* our Lord here by implication is stating
his confidence in the fact that the words written by Moses
1500 years before, had been transmitted correctly down the
centuries. *Second,* He is stating the fact that the original

writing of these words was the cause of their being in existence in His time. That could not be said of any writings other than the Word of God, for the mere act of writing something does not guarantee its preservation. In the use of the perfect tense here, there is an echo of the Psalmist's words, "Forever, O Lord, thy word is settled in heaven" (Psalm 119:89).

Or, take Paul's ἐστε σεσωσμένοι of Ephesians 2:8. The perfect participle will give you, "By grace were ye completely saved in past time, with the result that you are in a state of salvation at the present time." Taking up first the past time aspects of the perfect tense, we submit the following. If the participle had been aorist, the translation would read, "By grace ye were saved." That would merely speak of the fact that the person was saved in past time, but no details would be included in that statement. But when a Greek writer uses any other tense than the aorist, he goes out of his way to mention details by the use of the other tense. Here, not only is the fact referred to that the believer was saved in past time, but that the act of God in saving him was one that was complete. It lacked nothing to make it a perfect work. Nothing needed to be added. It was a complete salvation. That means that all of the believer's salvation was given him at the time he was saved, either actually or potentially. He was justified at the moment he put his faith in the Lord Jesus. The process of his sanctification was begun, to be continued all through his earthly life. His glorification in the eyes of God, as He viewed that believer in Christ, was also his (Rom. 8:30), although in actual experience it was his only potentially, but just as surely his forever as his justification and sanctification.

Taking up now the present aspect of the perfect tense, namely the present existing results of the past complete and finished act of saving him, we note that as a result of having accepted by faith a perfect salvation in past time, the believer is in the possession of that salvation in present time. This means that the assurance the believer has at any time that he is in a state of salvation is based upon the fact of his past acceptance of that salvation. Thus, the acceptance of salvation depends alone on the finished work of Christ on the cross, and the retention of that salvation depends alone upon the acceptance of that finished work.

But to make the case still stronger, Paul uses ἐστε in connection with the perfect participle, thus making the construction a periphrastic perfect. The perfect tense speaks of the *existence* of finished results in present time. The use of ἐστε adds durative force to the latter, making the compound construction speak of the *persistence* of finished results in present time. The full translation is, "By grace were you completely saved in past time, with the result that you are in a state of salvation which persists through present time." Paul could not have presented the eternal security of the believer in stronger language. The present results of the past action of the perfect in this case are always present with the reader.

Again, our Lord utters the cry, "It is finished" (John 19:30). John uses τετέλεσται in reporting it. Just before He died, in anticipation of what He would accomplish by that death, He cried, "It has been finished, and as a result it is in a finished state." One could translate, "It stands finished." Our Lord viewed His work of salvation wrought out on Calvary's cross as a finished work. He need not arise and, like the Levitical priests, repeatedly offer another sacrifice. His was a once-for-all sacrifice. The writer to the Hebrews says, "But this man, after he had offered one sacrifice for sins, sat down in perpetuity on the right hand of God" (10:12).

Thus, we have *a complete and perfect record* in the Word of God that is forever settled in heaven, of the salvation the believer is given, *a complete and perfect salvation* given the believer, and the believer's *complete and perfect retention* of the same for time and eternity. Observe how the use of the perfect tense in Scripture is in accord with the doctrine of the security of the believer as stated in such passages as John 10:27-30.

See the keen distinction in Romans 6:13 between the present imperative and the aorist imperative, the former referring to a continuous act, the latter to a once-for-all act. The translation reads, "Stop habitually putting your members at the service of sin as weapons of unrighteousness, but by a once-for-all act, put yourselves at the service of God." Here are scriptural grounds for a service where Christians are exhorted to dedicate themselves by a once-for-all act to God and His service. Such practical distinctions are lost to the student of the English Bible but readily available to the student of the Greek New Testament. A pastor, whom the writer had the privilege of tutoring in Greek, said one day, "My conscience hurts me if I do not use the Greek text in my preparation of messages." Surely, the Christian worker who has access to the Greek text cannot afford to neglect it. He does so at the expense of his own spiritual development and his efficiency in his service for the Lord Jesus.

In John 15:7, the words "ye shall ask" are aorist tense, imperative mood, and middle voice. A verb in the aorist tense and the imperative mood, issues a summary command given with military snap and curtness, a command to be obeyed at once. The Christian should not delay his asking. If he needs something that is in the will of God for him, he should ask at once. The imperative mood issues a command. This is no predictive future. The Lord commands us to pray for what we desire. Failure to do so is sin. Prayer is the appointed means through which God blesses us and supplies our needs. The voice here is indirect middle, which is defined as follows: *The subject of the verb in the indirect middle voice, acts in his own interest.* Thus, the Christian is commanded here to pray in his own interest, to ask for something for himself. See what a flood of light is thrown upon this verse by the simple application of the rules of Greek grammar. *But the point is, one must know those rules, and how to apply them.* This takes hard work and the fulness of the Holy Spirit. The Christian is the one to decide as to whether both of these will be true of him.

See Paul's trio of perfects in 2 Timothy 4:7, ἠγώνισμαι, τετέλεκα, τετήρηκα: "The desperate, straining, agonizing contest marked by its beauty of technique, I, like a wrestler have fought to a finish, and at present am resting in its victory. My race, I, like a runner, have finished, and at present am resting at the goal. The faith committed to my care, I, like a soldier, have kept safely through everlasting vigilance, and at present it is safely deposited in the keeping of my Captain." Observe Peter's use of the perfect in his first epistle (1:4), where the saint's inheritance has been kept guarded and is now in safe deposit in heaven for him. Touches like these add freshness, clearness, and power to the message of the preacher. They will bless his own soul and the lives of his hearers.

Some claim that the act of believing, referred to by the word "believe" in John 1:12, involves a continuous act of believing in order for one to accept and retain the salvation which God gives in response to the faith of the sinner. Others say that the word refers here only to the initial act of faith, and is descriptive of the one who exercises that faith. So far as the English translation here is concerned, this question could not be settled with any finality. But the Greek student can go to his kit of tools and bring out a few rules of Greek grammar that settle the question. The word "believe" is a present tense participle in the Greek text. The *aktionsart* of the present tense is durative, except where the context indicates that it is punctiliar. The durative action would give us, "to them who keep on continually believing on His Name." A glance at the context gives us ἔλαβον. The aorist tense as to *aktionsart* is punctiliar, referring to the fact of the action. The *fact* of receiving is expressed here. No process is referred to. Had there been a process of receiving Christ necessary for the acceptance and retention of salvation, the imperfect would have been used here, the *aktionsart* of which is durative. In that case, Paul would have used the present imperative when speaking to the Philippian jailor (Acts 16:31).

The conversation between the jailor and Paul took place in Greek. The jailor, being a Roman, would not be expected to know Aramaic. As a Roman official, and the responsible officer in charge of a Roman jail in a Greek city, he would have to know Greek. Paul spoke Greek to the chief captain who rescued him from the Jews, who, surprised that he could speak that language said, "Canst thou speak Greek?" (Acts 21:37).

The Philippian jailor said to Paul, "What is necessary in the nature of the case (δεῖ) for me to keep on continually doing (ποιεῖν) in order that I might be saved (σωθῶ)?" (Acts 16:30). Luke, a native Greek himself, inspired by the Holy Spirit to give an accurate report of this conversation as Paul had reported it to him, records the fact that the jailor used the present infinitive, which is durative in its *aktionsart* in contrast to the aorist infinitive which is punctiliar. When a Greek uses the present infinitive rather than the aorist, he is going out of his way to emphasize durative action.

From the use of the present infinitive by the jailor, we can learn something about his idea of how a man should be saved. It is the old pagan way of works: "What must I keep on doing in order to be saved?" The sinner must earn his salvation. And he can never have assurance of salvation, because he does not know how many good works he must do to be saved and how many he must keep on doing in order to keep saved. The jailor uses the aorist subjunctive when he says, "In order that I might be saved." Had he used the present subjunctive, the translation would be, "in order that I might keep on being saved," for the present subjunctive is durative in its *aktionsart*. The implication would be that he would have to keep on doing good works in order that those good works might keep on saving him. But in his use of the aorist subjunctive, he looked upon the salvation he would earn by his continual good works as a closed matter, since the aorist is the tense of finality. By his use of the aorist subjunctive, the jailor showed that he had no question as to the retention of his salvation, once it was his. He reasoned that if he was saved at all, he was saved. A salvation which could be lost was no salvation. The jailor's doctrine is therefore seen to be contradictory. Well, what answer did Paul give him? The jailor's idea of the method of the acceptance and retention of salvation was by a long-continued performance of good works.

Paul said, "Believe (πίστευσον) on the Lord Jesus Christ, and thou shalt be saved (σωθήσῃ)." He used the aorist imperative, referring merely to the fact of believing. Had a long continued process been involved, Paul would have been criminally remiss in his responsibility to this unsaved man when using the aorist, since the present imperative would have given the jailor the correct information as to the method of appropriating salvation, and the aorist imperative would have led him astray. When Paul speaks of salvation to him, he uses the future passive, which is built on the aorist stem. The future tense is *aoristic* in its *aktionsart.* Thus, Paul speaks of the finality of the gift of salvation. Therefore, the aorist tense used in John 1:12 and Acts 16:31 teaches us that it is the initial act of faith which results in one becoming a child of God forever.

Since the act of receiving the Lord Jesus as Savior is the same as the act of believing on His name, the word "believe" in John 1:12 cannot be durative but must be punctiliar, and therefore must refer to the initial act of placing one's faith in the Lord Jesus, not to a long continued process of believing. All of which means that the initial act of placing one's faith in the Lord Jesus results in one's possession and retention of salvation. Thus, the simple application of the rules of Greek grammar has solved another problem which in the English translation could not be solved.

See the flood of light that the present imperative throws upon the English translation of Matthew 7:7. The present imperative is definitely durative in its *aktionsart.* The Greek writer could easily choose the aorist imperative should he wish to speak merely of the fact of the action without adding details. The aorist tense is timeless in itself, and the present tense loses its time element when used in the potential moods. The Greek can therefore toss these about any way he chooses, since he is not hampered by time considerations.

The present imperative commands the doing of an action and its continuance. For instance, the Lord Jesus said of the man sick of the palsy, "Take up thy bed" (ἄρον), that is, "snatch up thy bed at once," "and walk" (περιπάτει), that is, "begin walking and keep on walking" (Mark 2:9). Here we have the aorist imperative issuing a peremptory command to be obeyed at once, and the present imperative, commanding the doing of the action and the continuing of that action. It was a permanent cure. When Jesus said, "Follow me" (Luke 18:22), the inspired writer reports His command in the present imperative (ἀκολούθει), "Start following me and keep on continually following me."

In Matthew 7:7, "ask," "seek," and "knock" are all in the present imperative. The translation reads, "Keep on asking and it shall be given you; keep on seeking and ye shall find; keep on reverently knocking and it shall be opened to you. For everyone who keeps on asking, keeps on receiving; and he that keeps on seeking, keeps on finding; and to him that keeps on reverently knocking, it shall be opened." See how intensely practical this translation is. A pastor on prayer-meeting night does not want to spend the time for a long Bible exposition, since the emphasis is on prayer. But he does want to bring his people a little spiritual food that will help make the prayer time what it should be. A brief hortatory message on a rich translation like this is just what he needs.

What practical lessons for everyday living and for one's prayer-life can be gotten out of this expanded translation? *First,* the text teaches perseverance in prayer. *Second,* it teaches that when we keep on praying, God keeps on working. *Third,* it teaches that if God does not answer our prayers at once, we are commanded to keep on asking in a reverent, humble way until He does, or until He shows us that the petition is not according to His will. Those and other practical lessons can be had from the simple application of a rule of Greek grammar. The saints will roll such choice morsels over their spiritual tongues to delight their spiritual gustatory nerves for days.

This presentation of the practical use of the Greek tense, mood, and voice, is merely illustrative. The Greek New Testament abounds with just such rich truth for the one who has eyes to see it, truth fresh with the dew of heaven upon it. The honey from heaven still drips from the comb. This is good energy food to whet the jaded appetites of the saints who listen to the same barrel of sermons year in and year out, given in the same way, without any fresh material and originality about them. The preacher who has a practical working knowledge of the Greek New Testament has so much fresh truth at his disposal and stored up in his heart and mind that he is hard pressed to find time and opportunity to give it all out. He can hardly wait until the next Lord's Day comes around to give his people some precious nugget of truth that the Holy Spirit has uncovered for him as he has studied his Greek text in preparation for his coming message. And when he comes into his pulpit on the Lord's Day morning, the saints in the pews can see by the expression on his face and the glow in his eye, that their pastor has received some fresh truth, some rich food for them during the week. They get a good square meal of spiritual food and are strengthened to live a more saintly life during the next week than they did the week before.

Dr. A. T. Robertson, in his book, *The Minister and His Greek New Testament*, has the following to say regarding the inexhaustible wealth of the Greek New Testament: "The Greek New Testament has a message for each mind. Some of the truth in it has never yet been seen by anyone else. It is waiting like a virgin forest to be explored. It is fresh for every mind that explores it, for those who have passed this way before have left it all here. It still has on it the dew of the morning and is ready to refresh the newcomer."

1. *Kind of action.*

4

The Practical Use of Prepositions

O NE OF THE things to which the student should pay particular attention is the matter of Greek prepositions. For instance, the usual interpretation of the words, "Who for the joy that was set before him endured the cross" (Heb. 12:2), is that our Lord in consideration of certain joy that would come to Him, endured the terrible ordeal of the cross. But such an interpretation is not in accord with other Scripture. If Philippians 2:5-8 means anything, it means that the considerations which led our Lord to go to the cross were utterly devoid of any thought of self. The Greek has it, "He emptied Himself." The word "Himself" is, in the Greek text, a pronoun in the accusative case. The action of the verb terminates upon the person or thing designated by the word in the accusative. The emptying terminated upon Himself. That is, our Lord emptied Himself of *self*. He set *self* aside. That means that His going to the cross was an absolutely self-less action. His attitude towards His work on the cross was

57

not even associated with any thought of joy that might accrue to Him by reason of His sufferings.

Furthermore, His going to the cross was in obedience to the Father's wishes. In the Gethsemane prayer, the words, "If it be possible, let this cup pass from me: nevertheless not as I will, but as thou wilt" (Matt. 26:39), and His words, "Lo, I come to do thy will, O God" (Heb. 10:9), plainly indicate that the consideration that led Jesus to become the sacrifice for sin, was a willing obedience to the Father's wishes. The interpretation of Hebrews 12:2 that states that the Lord Jesus went to the cross in order to obtain certain joy that was set before Him as an enticement urging Him on, is simply not correct in view of other Scripture statements.

Well, what is the student to do in a case like this? The process is simple. He will look up the preposition in the Greek text, and find ἀντί. The next thing he will do is to turn to Dana and Mantey on *Prepositions*,[1] and study ἀντί. The work of those scholars is based upon the papyri, and thus has the benefit of a first-hand knowledge of how the people of the first century used the Greek words found in the New Testament. They say that "There is conclusive proof now that the dominant meaning for ἀντί in the first century was *"instead of."* They give instances of this use in the LXX and in the New Testament. For instance, in Luke 11:11 we have, "Will he for (ἀντί instead of) a fish, give him a serpent?" The English preposition "for" has two uses. For instance, it is used in a sentence like this; "He worked all day long for his board and room." That is, in consideration of the fact that he would receive board and room for working, he worked all day. The other use is the one cited above.

Now, the point is that the student of the English Bible does not ask himself the question as to what two meanings the preposition "for" has, and consequently uses the one to which he is most accustomed, with the result, as in a case like this, that he arrives at an erroneous interpretation. But the Greek student is confronted with ἀντί, the meaning of which is clearly defined by its usage in the papyri, and he interprets the clause correctly.

The Greek could be translated here, "Who instead of the lying-before-Him joy." This takes us back to the time before our Lord's incarnation, when He had the joy of beholding the Father's face, of being the object of the adoration and worship of the angels, of being surrounded by the holiness and the beauties of heaven. *Instead of this joy* then present with Him, He came to earth, to be surrounded by the sin and squalor of human existence, to be the object of the hatred of man, and to have the Father turn away His face when He was hanging on the cross. This is far different from being urged on to the cross by considerations of reward. Thus, a careful study of the Greek preposition here discloses some precious truth that would otherwise be obscured by reason of a wrong interpretation put upon an English preposition, and at the same time saves the expositor from arriving at a wrong interpretation.

Take the difficult statement in Matthew 3:11, "I indeed baptize you with water unto repentance." The word "unto" means "result." For instance, "For I am not ashamed of the gospel, . . . for it is the power of God unto (resulting in) salvation" (Rom. 1:16). Are we to understand that a person's submission to water baptism results in his repentance? That is exactly what the King James Version says. But repentance is a supernatural work wrought in the heart of the seeking sinner by the Holy Spirit (Acts 11:18). It cannot therefore be a result of a mere ceremony.

The Greek student will find that the preposition εἰς appears in Matthew 3:11 and Romans 1:16. But prepositions in Greek are not confined to a single meaning in every context. Nor are they to be translated in a uniform way in their every occurrence in the Greek text.

A preposition has root meanings, resultant meanings, and remote meanings. It also has special meanings when used in composition with verbal forms. When the student is confronted with a problem like this, he should consult Dana and Mantey[2] on the word εἰς. Those scholars have classified the various uses of the prepositions in the New Testament. They also give illustrations of their various usages. For instance, they give μετενόησαν εἰς τὸ κήρυγμα Ἰωνᾶ (Matt. 12:41). Of course, one would not translate, "They (the men of Nineveh) repented unto the preaching of Jonah." That is, it would be ridiculous to say that the preaching of Jonah was the result of the repentance of the Ninevites. It was the other way round. They repented because of the preaching of Jonah. The Greek student would say here that this usage of εἰς would fit the context in which Matthew 3:11 is found. It would agree with the teaching of other Scriptures regarding the significance of water baptism. He would translate, "I indeed baptize you with water because of repentance." That is, repentance precedes water baptism, and baptism *is the outward visible* testimony of an inward fact, the person's repentance. Thus, another problem is solved, a difficulty removed, and an erroneous translation corrected, upon which translation is built the false doctrine of baptismal regeneration. We have the same difficulty in Acts 2:38. The same Greek preposition is used, and the same solution will meet the problem.

In Ephesians 3:17 we have, "that Christ may dwell in your hearts." κατοικῆσαι is the word translated "dwell." The word speaks of more than mere position. The verb οἰκέω means "to dwell," in the sense of making one's home in a certain place. The Greek word for "home" is οἶκος. The root meaning of the prefixed preposition κατά is "down." The idea of "down" gives one the conception of permanence. Looking up the first century usage of κατοικέω in Moulton and Milligan,[3] we find that this verb had a technical meaning. It referred to the permanent residents of a town as distinguished from those who lived there temporarily as strangers or sojourners. Thus, we have the wonderful truth brought out here by this Greek preposition that the Lord Jesus has come to the believer's heart to take up His permanent residence there. We have a related verb, κατοικίζω in James 4:5 that is also translated by the word "dwell." κατοικέω means "to make one's home in a certain place," κατοικίζω "to cause one to make one's home in a certain place." Thus, the fact of the permanent residence of the Holy Spirit in the heart of the believer, is brought out by the preposition κατά. *The idea of permanency would never occur to the student of the English Bible, but is clearly seen in the Greek text by the student who has eyes to see.* In passing, observe the meticulous accuracy with which the Holy Spirit selects those two Greek words. The Lord Jesus of His own volition takes up His permanent residence in the heart of the believer, but the Holy Spirit is caused to do so by God the Father in answer to the prayer of God the Son.

Hebrews 5:7 presents a difficulty. The fact is stated that our Lord Jesus prayed to be saved from death, and that His prayer was answered. That is simply not true. In the first place, it does not appear that in view of John 10:17-18, our Lord included in His Gethsemane prayer, the petition that He might be kept from dying a physical death. There was no adequate reason for such a request in view of the fact that He would arise again out from the state of death. The contents of the cup were *first,* the fact that He was to be made sin, and *second,* the fact that the Father would abandon Him when He was hanging upon the cross.

From those, the holy Son of God naturally shrank. However, if it be contended that He did pray at that time to be saved from dying, we must face the fact that His prayer was not answered. And Hebrews 5:7 says that it was. We face a like difficulty if we say that our Lord did pray that He might be spared from dying, and that His prayer was not recorded in the gospels. Granted for the moment that that was the case. We still are confronted with the fact that His prayer was not answered, and Hebrews 5:7 says it was.

Well, what can the student of the English Bible do about this? *He cannot do anything. He cannot offer a satisfactory explanation.* But the Greek student finds that the preposition translated "from" is ἐκ. He knows that there are two prepositions in the Greek language which mean "from," ἀπό, meaning "from the edge of," and ἐκ, meaning, "out from within." If the first were used, the petition would be to be saved from dying. If the second were used, it would be a prayer to be saved out from within death. That is, the petitioner would in that case fully expect to die, and in view of that fact, would pray to be raised out from the state of death. The use of ἐκ would mean that the petition would be one for resurrection.

Psalm 22 is thought by many to have been uttered by our Lord on the cross. Verses 1-13 describe His heart sufferings: verses 1-6, His heart sufferings caused by His abandonment by Deity, verses 7-13, His heart sufferings caused by His being spurned by man. Verses 14-18 describe His physical sufferings. Verses 19-21 are His prayer for resurrection, the one referred to in Hebrews 5:7. Verses 22-31 contain His thanksgiving and praise for answered prayer even before He received the actual answer, that of being raised out from death. Thus, a Greek preposition has solved an otherwise unsolvable problem, and has pointed the way to some precious truth regarding our

Lord Jesus. *The point is, that the student of the English Bible, and the Greek student who puts his Greek Testament away after he leaves the seminary, simply cannot cope with the problem. But the man who uses his Greek Testament not only solves the problem that the others could not solve, but is enabled to bring to his hearers rich truth to which the other expositor does not have access. People will wear a path to his church door, and the time and energy he would otherwise use in trying to corral them in he uses for deeper and more intensive study of the Greek New Testament. Hungry people go where they are fed rich, nourishing, spiritual food. The man who knows his Greek Testament always has more of that on hand than he has time or opportunity to give out.*

In Philippians 1:3, 5, Paul thanks God for the fellowship of the Philippian saints in the gospel. The word "fellowship" today is restricted almost exclusively in its meaning in church circles to the idea of companionship or social intercourse. The interpretation of this passage would be, therefore, that Paul was thanking God for the good times he had with the Philippians over the Word as he mingled with them.

The word "fellowship" is the translation of κοινωνία, which refers to the joint-participation two or more individuals have in a common purpose and activity. The preposition "in" is from εἰς, which is a preposition of motion and progress, as ἐν is a preposition of repose. Thus, Paul was thanking God for the Philippian's joint-participation with him in the progress of the gospel. He did not have reference here to his companionship with them in church meetings and Bible classes back in Philippi, but to their constant prayers and help as he went on his missionary journeys. They constituted the missionary-minded church that supported the missionary on the field.

Thus, a study of a little preposition like εἰς will bring to light some truth which otherwise would be missed in the English translation. This again shows that the Greek student is the more accurate expositor of the Word.

A Greek preposition prefixed to a verb has either one of two uses. There is the use in which the preposition adds an additional idea to the already existing idea in the verb; for instance, βάλλω, "I throw," ἐκβάλλω, "I throw out." This is called the local use. It fixes the locality within which the action of the verb is performed, or the direction the action of the verb takes. The other use is called the perfective use. Here the preposition does not add an additional idea to the verb, but intensifies the already existing idea. For instance: ἐσθίω, "I eat," and κατεσθίω, "I eat everything in sight."

An instance of the local usage which the King James Version misses is in Hebrews 12:2. The preposition ἀπό, which means "away from, off," is prefixed to the participle translated "looking." The saint is not only exhorted to look "unto" Jesus as he runs his life's race, but also "away" to Jesus. Paul is visualizing the stadium crowds, and the Greek runner who not only keeps his eyes fixed on the goal, but keeps his eyes away from the crowds. He runs entirely oblivious of the cheering, in some cases antagonistic crowds, for he knows that the slightest attention which he pays to them means that his speed is slackened by so much. So a Christian must run his life's race, entirely oblivious of onlookers. He must not serve the Lord Jesus to win their praise. He must not measure himself by their spiritual stature. He must not govern his choices by their opinions. His one duty is to keep his eyes on Jesus. The exhortation is, "Looking off and away to Jesus." Thus, a valuable and practical lesson in Christian racing technique, not at all brought out by the translation, is readily accessible to the one who knows his Greek Testament.

An instance of the perfective use of the preposition is found in Philippians 3:13. Paul is speaking of the Christian life as a race. He is writing to Greeks who were athletic minded. He says, "forgetting those things that are behind." The preposition ἐπί is prefixed to the verbal form "forgetting." This preposition in its local use means "upon." But here, in its perfective use, it merely intensifies the already existing idea in the verb. The exhortation is therefore, "completely forgetting those things that are behind." Paul knew Greek racing technique. He knew that the minute the Greek runner listened for the runners that were behind him in the race, and heard the thud, thud of their pounding feet, his speed would be slackened. He brings the lesson home to his readers, that he has made a complete break with his former life. To revert to that, even for a moment, would retard his speed in life's race. So with the Christian. He is to forget completely his past as long as it has been made right with God and man. How Satan likes to get us saints grieving over sins that have been forgiven and forgotten by God! He knows that our pace in life's race will be slackened. Thus, the simple application of a rule of Greek syntax has strengthened and made more effective a truth which, while given in the translation, did not have all the force in it which it possesses in the Greek text.

What a thrill comes to the Greek expositor when he examines the words in 1 Peter 5:10, "But the God of all grace who has called us unto his eternal glory," and discovers that the preposition εἰς has the following meanings in certain contexts, "with respect to, with reference to," thus, "with a view to." The English word "unto," so often used as the translation of εἰς, frequently hides some delicate and distinctive meanings of the latter. Now, since God has called the saints with a view to His eternal glory, that means that if He is to receive glory all through eternity from the fact that He has saved lost sinners, and from the fact that they in their likeness to the Lord Jesus redound to His glory, He must keep them in salvation. Should one be lost, He would be robbed by so much of the glory that would accrue to Him from that saint. God will not be robbed of His glory, which means that the person cleansed in Jesus' precious blood, regenerated by the Spirit, baptized by the Spirit into the Body of which Christ is the head, *will never be lost. All this added meaning comes from a little Greek preposition.*

Ephesians 3:9, 10 presents a problem in interpretation that is solved by a Greek preposition. Is Paul saying here that he has been given a revelation so that the wisdom of God even to the principalities and powers in heavenly places might be known by the church? The preposition "by" has that meaning. Or, does the apostle mean that this wisdom is made known to the principalities and powers by means of the church? The preposition "by" also has that meaning. The problem is easily solved by taking note of the Greek preposition involved. It is διά, the preposition of intermediate agency. The teaching is therefore that the wisdom of God is made known to the holy angels through the intermediate agency of the church. The church is the teacher of angels. *Where the English will huddle together in one word a number of meanings, the Greek will often allocate these meanings to as many separate words, thus making for clearness and distinctness of meaning.* The same preposition in John 1:3 shows that the Lord Jesus, when creating the universe, was not the absolute, independent creator, but the intermediate agent in creation.

The words, "All things were made by Him," would not give one this truth, but the preposition διά in the text here, clearly teaches that fact. *The student who uses his Greek Testament has access to more clearly presented truth than the student of the English Bible, and is therefore less liable to arrive at erroneous interpretations.*

In John 1:1, the word "with" is a good one-word translation of πρός. But it takes more than one word to bring out the full meaning of the Greek word. The root meaning of πρός is "near, facing." The preposition when used with persons implies a close fellowship between these persons. The "with" is not merely a "with" of proximity of position, but one of companionship, of mutual intercourse. Thus, the fellowship of God the Son with God the Father is brought out, a fellowship which existed in the eternity before the Son became incarnate. The student of the English Bible would normally pass over this preposition without particular comment simply because the English word "with" does not have such a full content of meaning that πρός has. All of which means that the student of the Greek New Testament will always have more to bring his hearers from any portion of the New Testament than the student of the English Bible, and for the reason that there is a great residue of untranslatable truth that still lies hidden away in the Greek text.

Prepositions may give one a vivid picture which is lost in the process of translation. In Acts 22:3, Paul tells his countrymen that he was brought up at the feet of Gamaliel. He could have used ἐν, πρός, or ἐπί, all meaning "at." He would then have had a position before the great teacher as he listened to him teach. But he chooses παρά, which means "beside," and which carries with it the idea of close personal association. Do you see the eager young man,

Saul, seated close to his teacher, *at his side,* drinking in every word that fell from his lips? This may be a very small touch, but it speaks volumes.

παρά is prefixed to the verb when the angel says to Joseph, "Take the young child and his mother and flee into Egypt" (Matt. 2:13). That is, "Take the young child and His mother to your side, under your protection." In John 1:11 we have, "Into the midst of His own things He came (His own universe, His own country, His own capital city, His own throne), and His own people did not reach out and take Him hospitably to themselves" (παρέλαβον). *Intimate, tender touches like these are lost to the English reader, but enrich the message of the Greek student.*

The preposition ὑπέρ means "over" (root meaning). In Romans 5:20 we have, "Where sin abounded, grace did much more abound." The Greek text is much stronger in its language. The words, "much more abound," are the translation of a verb meaning "to be over and above a certain number or measure, to be at hand in abundance, to be in superfluity, to be in affluence." That is, God's grace is in superabundance where sin abounds. There is more grace in God's heart, and available to the sinner through Calvary, than will ever be needed for a lost race. It is like the light and heat of the sun, of which a very small portion ever reaches this earth. But that is not all. Paul prefixes ὑπέρ to this verb, and thus says, "Where sin abounded, grace was in superabundance, *and then some on top of that.*" One could preach a good sermon on the subject, "God's Oversized Grace." There is available, through Calvary, enough grace to save the entire human race and keep it saved for time and eternity. But the sad note in it all is found in the words of the Lord Jesus, "And ye will not come to me, that ye might have life" (John 5:40).

The preposition ἐπί when used with the genitive case means "contact." John 6:19 reports our Lord as walking upon the sea. ἐπί with the genitive is used here. Our Lord's sandals actually had contact with the surface of the sea, as our shoes have contact with the hard pavement upon which we walk. The waves were high. That means that in order to reach the boat, He had to walk up and down a wave, and into the trough between that wave and the next. See what a literal, vivid picture this Greek preposition brings to one's mind. In Revelation 5:10, we have, "We shall reign on the earth." The same construction is used. That means that, during the millennial reign of the Lord Jesus, the glorified saints will have actual contact with this earth. We will walk on this earth as Jesus did in His glorified body.

These are a few examples of the possibilities of the practical use of Greek prepositions.

1. *Manual Grammar of the Greek New Testament,* p. 100.
2. *Manual Grammar of the Greek New Testament,* p. 104.
3. *Vocabulary of the Greek Testament.*

5
The Practical Use of
Synonyms

Archbishop Trench in commenting upon the study of synonyms says: "The value of this study as a discipline for training the mind into close and accurate habits of thought, the amount of instruction which may be drawn from it, the increase of intellectual wealth which it may yield, all this has been implicitly recognized by well-nigh all great writers. ... And instructive as in any language it must be, it must be eminently so in the Greek—a language spoken by a people of the subtlest intellect; who saw distinctions where others saw none; who divided out to different words what others often were content to huddle confusedly under a common term; who were themselves singularly alive to its value, diligently cultivating the art of synonymous distinction; and who bequeathed a multitude of fine and delicate observations on the right discrimination of their own words to the afterworld."[1]

Sometimes the keen distinction observed between two synonyms in the Greek New Testament will solve a problem with a finality that, without a knowledge of the Greek involved, could only receive a provisional and tentative answer based upon conjecture. For instance, what caused John the Baptist to doubt the Messiahship of the Lord Jesus (Matt. 11:3)? It could have been a bad case of prison sickness. Or it could have been the thought that, since Jesus did not get him out of prison, He was helpless to do so, and in that case He would not be the supernatural Messiah the Old Testament predicted. And so one could go on devising reasons for John's defection, plausible in themselves but not final, since they are based on conjecture and not on what is written.

A synonym in the Greek text solves the problem easily. John sends two of his disciples with this question, "Art thou he that should come, or do we look for another?" The expression, "he that should come" is Jewish, referring to the Messiah whom Israel was expecting in fulfillment of Old Testament prophecy. The particular synonym translated "another," gives us the clue that leads us to the solution of our problem. There are two words in Greek, each meaning *another*, ἕτερος and ἄλλος. ἕτερος means *another of a different kind*, ἄλλος, *another of the same kind*.

ἕτερος denotes qualitative difference; ἄλλος, numerical difference. ἕτερος distinguishes one of two. ἄλλος adds one besides. ἕτερος involves the idea of difference of kind, whereas ἄλλος denotes simply distinction of individuals. Thus, John asked, "Art thou he that should come, or do we look for another of a different kind?" Here is our clue. John expected a Messiah of a different kind than Jesus was. He had up to now believed that Jesus was the Messiah. He had learned that from his mother Elizabeth, who in turn had learned it from Mary. He had recognized Jesus as Messiah when He had come to him for baptism. He had had the sign of the Father's voice from heaven, and had seen the descent of the Holy Spirit upon Jesus. He had announced Him as both Messiah and Lamb of God, the first title speaking of Him as King of Israel, the second, as the One who would die for the sins of mankind. But now, with all that evidence, he doubted His Messiahship.

Jesus did not fit John's picture of Messiah. He had preached a Messiah of judgment (Matt. 3:10-12). Jesus had forgiven sins, cleansed the leper, healed the sick, ministered to the poor. John knew that he had his message from God, and that his description of Messiah had therefore come from the same source. The fact that Jesus did not fit that picture, caused John to doubt His Messiahship. Had John been alive when Jesus gave Jerusalem and Israel over to judgment (Matt. 23:37-39), he would have seen that He did fit that picture. Thus, a simple study of synonyms in the Greek text, has answered a question which is not easily answered by the student of the English Bible.

Take the meaningless juggling of Paul's words in the King James Version of Galatians 1:6, 7, where he speaks of "another gospel which is not another." How could the message of the Judaizers be another gospel if it was not another gospel? It is all a mystery to the English reader. But one glance at this passage by the Greek student, gives him "another ἔτερος gospel which is not another ἄλλος gospel." His reaction is as follows: Paul calls the message of the Judaizers, a gospel of a different character from the gospel of grace, and a gospel which will not serve as an alternative gospel. That makes sense. Here is just another example of the untranslatable clarity of some parts of the Greek New Testament. A nice distinction like this is entirely lost upon the expositor of the English translation.

The English language is not equipped to handle some of these delicate distinctions found in the Greek, without devoting a sentence or a whole paragraph sometimes in the attempt to translate the thought of the original. And this is not permitted in a standard translation. There are undreamed of possibilities of interpretation of which the expositor is entirely oblivious as he studies the English Bible, which are easily accessible to the one who will take the trouble to work in the Greek New Testament. ἕτερος is used 99 times, and ἄλλος, 257 times in the New Testament. This means that in these 356 places, the student of the English Bible fails to obtain a full-orbed, complete interpretation. His interpretation may be approximately correct, but it cannot be as clear cut and exact as that of the one who works in the Greek Testament.

The statement of John the Baptist, twice repeated, "I knew him not" (John 1:31, 33), presents a real difficulty in the English translation. John's statement here is to the effect that he did not know Jesus as Messiah of Israel when He came for baptism, and it was only the miracle of the Father's voice from heaven and the descent of the Spirit who rested upon Him, that caused John to recognize Him as such. But certainly John knew Jesus as Messiah, for he kept on hindering Him when He was asking for baptism, saying, "I have need to be baptized of thee, and comest thou to me?" He knew Him as the coming Messiah since he was a boy, for his mother Elizabeth was related to Mary. Both of those women knew that Jesus would be Messiah and John would be His forerunner. That information they certainly imparted to their sons. John had pointed Jesus out as He was coming for baptism, identifying Him as the Lamb of God.

Well, what can the student of the English Bible do with such a contradiction? *Absolutely nothing.* But the Greek student is acquainted with the synonyms, γινώσκω and οἶδα, the first referring to knowledge gained by experience, the second, to absolute, intuitive, and self-evident knowledge. οἶδα is used here. John had known of the Messiahship of Jesus through experience. But not until he heard the voice from heaven and had seen the Holy Spirit descend upon Him, did he have absolute proof of the same. John's belief that Jesus was the Messiah lacked that full and entire assurance which the predicted sign gave him, and which the word οἶδα implies, which assurance would justify him in announcing Him as Messiah. Thus, another difficulty is cleared up that would remain unsolved in the English translation. γινώσκω is used 220 times, and οἶδα, 296 times. This means that in order to arrive at a full-orbed, meticulously accurate interpretation of 516 places in the New Testament where these synonyms appear, the student ought to know his Greek and use it. Those delicate distinctions, sometimes throwing a flood of light upon the interpretation of the passage, are denied the English reader.

In John 13:6-10, νίπτω, *to wash part of the body*, and λούω, *to perform a complete ablution*, are entirely hidden to the English reader, with the consequent loss of the real point of the whole passage. νίπτω is used in verses 6 and 8, and at the second occurrence of the word "wash" in verse 10. λούω is also translated "wash" in the other instance of the English word in verse 10. λούω is in the perfect tense here. The translation reads: "He that hath been completely bathed is as a present result in a completely bathed condition, and needs not except to wash his feet, but is clean every whit." The oriental background here is that of the Roman baths, where the Roman would perform a complete ablution (λούω). But by the time he reached his home, his feet would be dusty, and he would have his slave wash (νίπτω) them. He stayed bathed until he reached home, and

did not need λούειν but only νίπτειν. So the believer is
λελουμένος, completely washed from his sins at Calvary,
but as he walks through this life, sin at times enters his
experience. He need not go back to the cross to be bathed
(λούω) all over again in the fountain filled with blood, for
he stays bathed until he reaches heaven. But he needs to
confess that sin, and be washed (νίπτω) from the defilement
which that sin brought into his life. Such clear, rich,
accurate truth is entirely lost to the English reader, since
the translations do not distinguish between synonyms that
appear in the Greek text.

Another instance where synonyms appear in juxtaposition in the Greek text and are not distinguished in the
translation is in Ephesians 4:12-13, where the word "perfecting" in verse 12 is the translation of a Greek word, the
meaning of which is entirely different from the Greek
word translated "perfect" in verse 13. The expositor of the
English Bible, entirely ignorant of this fact, cannot offer a
full-orbed, accurate interpretation of this passage. Too
often we use Bible terms without explaining them. A
perfect Christian is a perfect Christian, that is all. Or, a
perfect Christian is a flawless, sinless Christian, if an
interpretation is offered.

The Greek student at a glance sees that "perfecting" in
verse 12 is the translation of καταρτίζω which refers to the
equipping of a Christian for Christian service, and τέλειος
in verse 13 refers to the spiritual maturity of a Christian.
This throws a flood of light upon the passage. The pastor
should specialize in equipping the Christians in his
congregation to do Christian work, so that the saints will
be built up in their Christian lives and thus become
spiritually mature. *The full significance of such an important passage like this, which deals with the God-ordained
way in which a pastor should minister in his church and*

with the responsibility of the saints also to engage in Christian work, is lost to the student of the English Bible, simply because synonyms that occur in the Greek text are not handled in the translation. τελειόω and its various forms occurs 37 times where it is translated by the word "perfect," καταρτίζω 9 times.

One of the richest, most prolific sources of truth is the careful distinction which should be maintained with respect to the two words for "love" in the New Testament, ἀγπάω and φιλέω. And yet, the translations make no distinction between them. But we cannot blame the translators for that, since it is impossible in a standard translation which is held down to a minimum of words, to bring out this distinction. Yet those expositors of the Word who have been given training in Greek lay themselves open to severe censure if they neglect their Greek New Testament. *An enormous amount of rich truth is lost by one's neglect of the Greek synonyms.*

The statement of our Lord in John 21:18, regarding the manner of Peter's death, is absolutely unrelated to the preceding context unless one differentiates between the two Greek words used for "love" in the conversation of Jesus and Peter. ἀγαπάω, which Jesus uses twice, is a love of devotion. φιλέω, which Peter uses three times, and our Lord uses once, is a love of emotion. ἀγαπάω is a love that impels one to sacrifice one's self for the one loved. φιλέω is a fondness, an affection having no ethical content. ἀγαπάω is the word used when the Bible writers speak of the love that the Holy Spirit produces in the heart of the yielded saint. This is the kind of love Jesus expected of Peter. All Peter offered him was a human fondness and affection. The Lord Jesus says in effect, "Never mind, Peter, some day you will have an ἀγαπάω love for Me, and you will show it by dying a martyr's death on a Roman cross."

There is the vital connection between our Lord's statement with respect to the martyr death of Peter, and the conversation which went before.

When Paul says, "Husbands, love your wives" (Eph. 5:25), he uses ἀγαπάω. They already had a human fondness for them (φιλέω), or they would not have married them. And the ἀγαπάω love with which they are to love their wives is defined as to content in 1 Corinthians 13. *That kind of truth enriches the sermon of the pastor and makes it all the more powerful and effective.*

See the meticulous care with which the Holy Spirit guards the character of the Lord Jesus through His choice of these synonyms. The sisters said, "Lord, behold, he of whom thou art fond (φιλέω) is sick." But when John speaks of the love of Jesus for Martha and Mary, he uses ἀγαπάω, the word for a divine love that is as pure as the beam of light down which the Holy Grail travelled in the vision of Sir Galahad.

When John speaks of the fondness and affection which God the Father has for God the Son, he uses φιλέω (John 5:20). What a precious thought the Greek student finds in John's use of φιλέω (John 16:27), when he speaks of the fondness and affection which the Father has for those Christians who are fond of the Lord Jesus, and who have an affection for Him in their hearts. And the more fondness there is in the heart of a Christian for the Lord Jesus, the more fondness the Father has for that Christian. *Touches like these are lost to the student of the English Bible, who would naturally interpret this love to be the love of God exhibited at Calvary's cross.* We have not presented a detailed definition of these words here, since we are not dealing with word studies in this chapter, but with the practical value of the study of synonyms. When we learn that ἀγαπάω is used in its various forms of verb, noun, and adjective about 320 times in the New Testament, and φιλέω 45 times, we can begin to realize what a tremendous amount of truth is at the disposal of the expositor who uses his Greek Testament, which is entirely lost to the student of the English Bible.

There are three Greek words in the New Testament translated by the one English word "world," κόσμος, αἰών and οἰκουμένη. It should be obvious that if one is to arrive at a full-orbed, accurate interpretation of the passages where the word "world" is found, one must know which Greek word is used, and the distinctive meaning of that Greek word.

Trench, contending for the use of "world" as the proper translation of κόσμος, and "age" as the correct rendering of αἰών says: "One must regret that, by this or other device, our translators did not mark the difference between κόσμος, the world contemplated under aspects of space, and αἰών, the same contemplated under aspects of time." κόσμος is used to refer to the world system, wicked, and alienated from God, yet cultured, educated, powerful, outwardly moral and religious—the system in which Satan is the head, the fallen angels and the demons are his servants, and all mankind other than the saved are his subjects. This includes those people, pursuits, pleasures, purposes, and places where God is not wanted. It also refers at times to the universe, and to the human race.

Trench defines αἰών as follows: "All that floating mass of thoughts, opinions, maxims, speculations, hopes, impulses, aims, aspirations, at any time current in the world, which it may be impossible to seize and accurately define, but which constitute a most real and effective power, being the moral or immoral atmosphere which at every moment of our lives we inhale, again inevitably to exhale." He says, "All this is included in the αἰών which is, as Bengal has expressed it, the subtle, informing spirit of the κόσμος or world of men who are living alienated and apart from God."

οἰκουμένη referred in classical Greek to that portion of the earth inhabited by the Greeks, as opposed to the rest of the earth where non-Greeks or barbarians lived. Later, the word was used to designate the entire Roman Empire.

κόσμος is used by Paul to designate the material universe, and since it means "an ordered system" as against χάος, "a rude unformed mass," it speaks of the fact that the original state of the universe was one of perfection (Acts 17:24). John tells us that God loved the κόσμος (the human race). He also tells us that we should not love the κόσμος (the world system of evil) (1 John 2:15). Peter speaks of the κόσμος (the adornment) of the Christian woman (1 Peter 3:3). αἰών is used by our Lord when He speaks of this αἰών (age) and that αἰών (age) which is to come. He is not speaking here of this present existence as compared to the existence after death, as might be inferred from the use of the word "world," but of this present age and the millennial age to come (Matt. 12:32). Paul says that the Lord Jesus gave Himself for our sins that He might deliver us from this present evil αἰών (age) (Gal. 1:4).

There is significance in the use of οἰκουμένη in the statement that Paul and his associates had turned the world upside down (Acts 17:6). The impact of Christianity had been felt throughout the Roman Empire. The census ordered by Caesar Augustus was to include the οἰκουμένη, the entire Roman Empire (Luke 2:1). The word means literally "the inhabited earth." The context must rule as to what portion of the inhabited earth is referred to. For instance, its use in Luke 2:1 limits the reference to the Roman Empire, but its use in Hebrews 2:5 includes the entire earth, for the millennial empire of the Lord Jesus will be worldwide. In Hebrews 1:6, the Lord Jesus, who created the world (κόσμος), is said to come into the world (οἰκουμένη), the inhabited world.

Κόσμος is used 187 times in the New Testament, αἰών, 38 times where it is translated by the word "world," and οἰκουμένη, 14 times. But the point is, that the keen distinctions among these three words are obscured by the King James Version, with the result that the expositor who confines himself to that translation simply does not arrive at a full-orbed and absolutely accurate interpretation of the passages in which these words are found. Hence, a knowledge of the Greek text is essential if the expositor expects to do the highest type of work.

Take the word "blessed" for instance. That is the uniform translation of μακάριος and εὐλογητός, two entirely different Greek words. The former, where used to describe the believer, means "spiritually prosperous." For instance, "Spiritually prosperous are the pure in heart: for they shall see God" (Matt. 5:8). Or this; "There is more spiritual prosperity in constantly giving than in constantly receiving" (Acts 20:35).

On the other hand, εὐλογητός, made up of εὖ "well" and λέγω "to speak," means "to speak well of, to praise." Our words "eulogize" and "eulogy" are derived from this word. Paul uses it in Ephesians 1:3, ("Blessed be the God and Father of our Lord Jesus Christ"), in the sense that God is worthy of being well-spoken of, of being eulogized. He uses it also in the words, "Who hath blessed us." Thus, when man blesses God, it is an exaltation with words. When God blesses man, it is an exaltation by act, that of conferring benefits upon him.

Too often we use words in the New Testament without being sure that we know their content of meaning. We have a rather hazy idea as to what they mean, and let it go at that. We say "Blessed are the meek," "blessed be God," and "who hath blessed us," without carefully distinguishing the content of meaning in each case. This makes for shallow, surface exposition that lacks the clarity, power, and simplicity which a knowledge of the Greek synonyms would give one. μακάριος occurs 43 times, εὐλογητός, 52 times. One simply cannot neglect the Greek text in the case of synonyms if he expects really to come to grips with the meaning of the passage where the particular synonym occurs.

1. *Synonyms of the New Testament, Trench, preface, p. vi.*

6
The Practical Use of Word Studies

T HE ENGLISH language is totally inadequate to offer a full-orbed translation of some of the words in the Greek New Testament, and for the reason that it does not contain words whose content of meaning is equal to the total content of meaning of the Greek words. The best it can do is to reproduce the main idea in the Greek word, and content itself with that, leaving in the Greek text the details that cluster around the main idea.

For instance, the word "form" is the best English word which will translate the word μορφή. But it is most inadequate. This word usually means "shape." But μορφή does not mean that. The word "form" is used in Philippians 2:6, 7, in the phrases, "who being in the form of God," and, "took upon him the form of a servant." The meaning, "shape," will not do here. The word "form" is sometimes interpreted here as referring to a station in life, a position one holds, one's rank. And that is an approximation of μορφή in this context. The word is used in this way when a certain grade in school is spoken of as a form. The meaning of these phrases then would be that our Lord was, as to His rank or position, Deity previous to His incarnation, and that he had the rank or position of a servant during His earthly life.

This is all true. But see how far short this comes of the total content of meaning in the Greek word. μορφή is a Greek philosophical term referring to the outward expression one gives of his inward nature, that outward expression proceeding from and being truly representative of that inward nature. The words, "being in the form of God," refer to our Lord's being in that state of being in which He gives outward expression of His inner essence of Deity, that outward expression proceeding from and being truly representative of His inner intrinsic essence.

The words, "took upon him the form of a servant" refer to Him during His incarnation, giving outward expression of His inner nature as a servant, that outward expression proceeding from and being truly representative of His inner nature, that of Deity desiring to serve. The words do not refer to our Lord's assumption of humanity. The latter He used as a medium through which He served.

Now, when the word "form" is understood as meaning "rank" or "station," the passage is made to teach that our Lord exchanged one station or rank for another. He was in the rank or station of Deity before He became incarnate, but when He came to earth, He took the rank or station of a servant. And that is all true so far as it goes. But the question of the essential nature of the Lord Jesus, that of Deity, is not touched. Did He cease to be Deity when He became a servant? Theological liberalism would have it so.

But when the full-orbed meaning of μορφή is brought into the picture, we have "being in that state of being in which He gave outward expression of His inner nature, that of Deity," and "took upon Him the outward expression of a servant, which outward expression was (also) that of His inner nature." We use the word "form" in this way when we say, "The tennis-player's form was excellent." We mean that the outward expression he gave of his inner ability to play tennis was excellent. This means that the outward expression our Lord gave of Himself was changed, both expressions coming from Him as Deity, and that while His rank on earth was that of a servant, yet He was Very God of Very God while in His incarnation. *Thus, a study of μορφή gives us the full and adequate understanding of a passage which is imperfectly understood by the student who has only the English Bible at his disposal.*

The word "being" (Phil. 2:6), is an inadequate translation of ὑπάρχων. The English word refers only to the time denoted by the context, the context here speaking of our Lord's pre-incarnate state. But ὑπάρχων refers to an antecedent condition protracted into the present. The English word, "being," speaks of our Lord in the form of God in His pre-incarnate state. But ὑπάρχων refers that state of being not only to the time previous to His coming to earth, but asserts that our Lord was in that state at the time Paul was writing to the Philippians. That means that our Lord, when taking upon Himself the outward expression of a servant, did not relinquish His deity, for He was giving expression to that in His glorified humanity. This one word is enough to refute the contention of theological liberalism to the effect that, when our Lord emptied Himself, He emptied Himself of His deity. But the point is, that one does not get all this from the word "being," but from ὑπάρχων. *All of which goes to say that the English language is not equipped to give the full meaning of some of the Greek words in the New Testament, and if the student expects to arrive at a full-orbed interpretation of those passages where these words occur, he simply must know the Greek text of those passages.*

We have μεταμορφόομαι in Matthew 17:2. The best the English language can do is to give us the word "transfigure," which Webster defines as follows: "to change the form or appearance of." What we have in the translation is the fact that our Lord's outward appearance was changed. And that is true. But see how much more we get from the Greek word. μορφή referred, you remember, to the outward expression one gives of his inner nature, that outward expression proceeding from and being representative of that inner nature. μορφόομαι refers therefore to the act of giving outward expression to that nature, that outward expression proceeding from and being truly representative of that nature. The verb here is in the passive voice. μετά, when prefixed to a verb, signifies a change. Thus, we translate "The mode of His outward expression was changed before them, that outward expression proceeding from and being truly representative of His inner nature." Our Lord's usual outward expression on earth, while in His humiliation, was that of a bondservant. But now, the glory of the essence of His deity came from the depths of His inmost nature, and shone through the clay walls of His humanity. You simply will not get all that out of the word "transfigure," even though you look up its meaning in Webster's Unabridged. All of which means that the English language is not equipped to handle the total meaning of some of the Greek words in the New Testament, with the result that much rich truth is left behind in the process of translating, truth which the average audience seldom if ever hears because of the ignorance of the Greek text on the part of so many preachers of the Word.

Or, take μετασχηματίζω in 2 Corinthians 11:13-15, translated by the word "transform." Each occurrence is in the direct middle voice. The false apostles transform themselves into the apostles of Christ. Satan transforms himself into an angel of light. His ministers transform themselves into ministers of righteousness.

The Greek verb means "to transform one's self," but it means more than that. It refers to the action of changing one's outward expression by assuming an outward expression which does not come from within, and is not representative of one's inner nature, while all the time there is no change in one's inner nature. It is an outward change of that which inwardly remains the same. That is the full content of meaning in this Greek word translated by the one word "transform." Of course, the translators were held down to a minimum of words, and we could not expect them to give the total meaning of the Greek word in such a translation. And right here is where the student should use his Greek text.

Satan originally was an angel of light, and the enswathement of light that clothed his person came from his inner nature. This is μορφόομαι. But he fell into sin and gave outward expression of the darkness of his totally depraved nature. This is also μορφόομαι. But he saw that he could not deceive and attract the human race in that way. So he changed his outward expression to that of an angel of light by assuming from the outside an expression of light, that expression not coming from nor being representative of his sin-darkened nature. This is μετασχηματίζω. The word "masquerade" would be an approximation of the total content of this word. But even that does not translate the word in its fulness.

When we look at Romans 12:2 we find that the translators have given us the same word "transform" for μεταμορφόομαι, a word that means the exact opposite of μετασχηματίζω. Both refer to an outward transformation, but each speaks of a different and diametrically opposed method of bringing that expression about. All this is lost to the expositor who is limited to, or limits himself to, the English translation. The word "conformed" is the translation offered of συσχηματίζω. It is the best one can do in a single English word. But see the wealth of meaning in the Greek word, which is left behind in the Greek text by the translators. The word means "to assume an outward appearance which does not come from within, nor is it representative of one's inner nature, but is patterned after something else."

What surface exposition is done on the basis of the English translation, good and correct in itself, is abysmally inadequate in many instances. Given two men of equal abilities, filled with the Spirit, the one who uses his Greek text is always the more accurate and able expositor of the Word. The Holy Spirit does the best He can with what the preacher gives Him. When the preacher brings to his study the tools of scholarship, the Holy Spirit is able to lead him into more, deeper, and clearer truth than He can the one who confines himself to the translations. Greek is the most excellently equipped of the various languages spoken by man, and that is one of the reasons why God chose it for the New Testament language.

The preacher may be looking for material for an evangelistic sermon, and his eye lights on Romans 6:16-17 as a Scripture portion that speaks of the contrast between the unsaved and the saved, the former, servants of sin, the latter, servants of righteousness. He considers the word "servant" and gets this: "a voluntary employee working for a stipulated salary, who can quit any time he wants to." But he reflects that the unsaved person is compelled to serve Satan by reason of his fallen nature. He has no choice in the matter. Furthermore, the unsaved person

never stipulates the wages he receives, death, sorrow, heart-
ache, suffering. Again, the unsaved person cannot say to
Satan, "I am through. I'm quitting." There is not much
food for an evangelistic message in that. All of which goes
to say that the current meaning and usage of the word
"servant" does not fit the Pauline doctrine of total
depravity.

But, let the preacher turn to his Greek New Testament,
and he has δοῦλος. He studies the word in various lexicons
and word studies, and finds the following: A δοῦλος is one
born into slavery, as against an ἀνδράποδον, a person taken
in war, or a freeman who is kidnapped and made a slave.
And he says, "There is the first point in my message. A
sinner is born into slavery to sin by his first birth. He is
born into a loving, willing bond-service to the Lord Jesus
by the new birth. By one stroke, I have divided my audience
into two classes, the unsaved and the saved, and I have
caused the unsaved to see their unsaved condition more
clearly by contrast, and have shown them that they are not
children of God because they are not born again." With
this he will explain the necessity of the atonement and of a
personal faith in the Lord Jesus.

Then he studies δοῦλος further. He finds that the word
refers to a slave that is in a permanent relationship to his
master which only death can break. He says, "There is my
second point. The believing sinner's identification with
Christ in His death, severed his relationship to Satan. I
will take my audience into Romans Six. And because
Christ will never die again, the believer will never die, for
Christ is his life. And I will go into Romans 8."

Then he pursues his study of δοῦλος a little further. He
finds that it refers to one whose will is swallowed up in
the will of another. And he says, "There is my third point.
Before salvation, the person's will is swallowed up in the

will of Satan. After believing, his will is swallowed up in the sweet will of God. I will dwell upon the blessedness of salvation, its opportunity of fellowship with the Lord Jesus, of service for Him, of the peace and satisfaction that comes from living a Christian life." His subject will be, "Whose Slave are You, Satan's or God's?"

Now, the point is, that as long as he had the word "servant" staring him in the face, he got nothing but a few ideas not at all in harmony with the rest of Scripture. But, the minute δοῦλος came before his eyes, it challenged him to investigation and study, from which proceeded fresh, rich, clear, positive truth that suggested a message with something original in it, and for the reason that he went back to origins for it.

Or, take this illustration of the way a look at the original text gives one a fresh, new approach to a message. The pastor is looking for some material for a simple, heart-to-heart message for the saints on prayer-meeting evening. He is reading Paul's prayer in Ephesians 3:14-21, and he comes to the words, "That Christ may dwell in your hearts." He thinks: "Paul must be referring to something more than the residence of the Lord Jesus in the heart. The Lord Jesus is in every saint's heart. What is back there in the Greek text?" And he finds κατοικῆσαι. At once he gets out his Greek tools and goes to work. *Watch him work now.* First, οἰκέω has the same stem as οἶκος, the word for "home." οἰκέω means therefore "to live in a certain place as one's home," thus, "to make one's home there." In a context like this it could mean, "to live in the heart of the Christian, make one's home there, feel at home there." Second, the tense is aorist, culminative aorist as to classification. This latter emphasizes the completion of an action. Third, the aorist tense is the tense of finality. Fourth, the prefixed preposition κατά means "down" (root meaning), and adds the idea of permanence to the already existing idea in the verb. Indeed, Moulton and Milligan in their *Vocabulary of the Greek Testament* say that κατοικέω was used as a technical term designating the permanent residents of a town in contrast to the temporary ones. With these four ideas before me, I will proceed to the fuller or expanded translation of this word. The King James Version uses one word "dwell" to translate this word. I am not limited to one word, and so I will translate, "That Christ may finally settle down and feel completely at home in your hearts." My subject will be, "Does Jesus Feel at Home in My Heart?" The context speaks of the ministry of the Holy Spirit enabling the saint to make the Lord Jesus feel at home, and so I will not only exhort my people to make the Lord Jesus feel at home in their hearts, but I will tell them how to do that thing. And so the pastor has a precious nugget of truth, fresh from the Greek New Testament, something new, with an approach which his people have never seen.

Or see how one Greek word will give the preacher an idea which can be developed into a graphic and clear illustration of the relationship of the sinning saint to the Lord Jesus. The pastor is working in the Greek text of Galatians 6:1. Paul is speaking of some saints who had been overtaken by sin in their lives. The Spirit-filled saints are exhorted to restore these. The word "restore" is the translation of καταρτίζω. The latter has the idea of setting someone to rights, of bringing him into line. These sinning saints needed to be set to rights, to be brought into line. The pastor finds that one of its uses was "to put a dislocated arm back in joint." At once there flashes across his mind the fact that the human body and the human head are used in Ephesians as illustrations of the relationship of the church to the Lord Jesus. Each saint is a member of the Body of which Christ is the Head. He says, "I have it. I will preach on 'Dislocated Saints.' My points will be drawn from the relationship of a dislocated arm to the body of which it is a member, and to the head of that body. Just as a dislocated arm is still a member of the human body, so the sinning saint is still a member of the Body of Christ. Just as the life-blood that flows through the head is still flowing through the arm, so the life of the Head, Jesus Christ, is still the possession of the saint. Just as a dislocated arm is most painful, so a sinning saint is most miserable. Just as a dislocated arm is useless to the head, so a sinning saint is useless to the Lord Jesus. Just as a dislocated arm refuses to obey the head, so a sinning saint refuses to obey his Head, the Lord Jesus. Just as a dislocated arm will not work in cooperation with the other members of the body, so a sinning saint will not work in cooperation with other Christians. Just as a dislocated arm is harder to put back in joint the longer it is out of joint, so it is harder to get a Christian back in fellowship with his Lord, the longer he is out of fellowship. Just as it is easier for an arm to slip out of joint the oftener it is dislocated, so it is easier for a Christian to sin, the oftener he sins. Just as a person cannot put his dislocated arm back in joint himself, but needs a physician to do that for him, so a child of God cannot put himself back into fellowship with the Lord Jesus, but must go to the great Physician of souls, confess that sin, be cleansed from its defilement in the precious blood, and be restored by his Lord."

Such a graphic and plain illustration will not be lost on the saints. After all, it is the simple, plain, sometimes homely presentation of the truth which is most effective. But the point is that such an illustration would never occur to the pastor as he reads the word "restore." But let him study καταρτίζω, and it will jump at him. This is the value of Greek word studies.

The habit of not being satisfied with the English word and, as a consequence, going back to the Greek text, will often keep a Bible expositor from some rather humiliating blunders. It gives one pause to hear learned expositors of the Word refer to the fact that Peter used profanity ("He began to curse and to swear," Mark 14:71) when he denied the Lord Jesus. That is an evidence of two things. First, it is an evidence of the fact that we often interpret some of the words in the translation in their current usage, which latter is sometimes quite divergent from that of A.D., 1611. Second, it is clear evidence of the fact that the expositor has not consulted the Greek text. Of course, the words "curse and swear" today are used commonly to refer to profanity. But two things must always be fixed in the mind of the one who undertakes to teach God's Word, and that is that the King James Version (which most people still use), is of 1611 vintage, and that the Greek text is interpreted with the aid of the contemporary usages of the words it contains. We turn to the Greek text of Mark 14:71, and we find that the word "curse" is ἀναθεματίζω, "to declare anathema or accursed, to devote to destruction." Paul used the same word in Galatians 1:8-9. In this passage it means "to asseverate with direful imprecations." Peter, in his act of disclaiming any connection with Jesus, enforced his statement by calling down upon himself the divine curse, if what he was saying was not true, quite a different thing from using profanity. The word "swear" is the translation of ὀμνύω "to swear, to affirm, to promise or threaten with an oath." It is the same word used when God is said to swear (Heb. 6:13). God took an oath upon Himself that what He said was true. Just so, Peter took an oath to the effect that he was telling the truth. *It does not*

*take much time to look up words like these, and one is a
far more accurate expositor of the Word when he does.*

Take the word "vain" (Rom. 1:21). The words "vain"
and "vanity" today are used to refer to pride. The unsaved
are said to have become vain in their reasonings. The
interpretation is therefore that they were filled with pride.
But the word in the Greek text does not mean that. The
word is ματαιόω. One glance at the *papyri*[1] usage of this
word and its cognates, gives us phrases such as, "he *vainly*
relates," "*useless* expense." The word "suggests either
absence of purpose or failure to attain any true purpose."
A better translation today would be "they became those
whose reasonings were futile." Take Romans 8:20, "For
the creation was made *subject to vanity*." That is, in the
curse, the perfect universe was rendered futile, unable to
fulfill the purpose for which it was brought into being.
The purposes which God had for the universe, were rendered relatively futile by the curse. In 1 Peter 1:18, the
apostle reminds us that the recipients of the letter were not
redeemed from their vain (futile) conversation (manner of
life). That is, their manner of life was futile in that it did
not measure up to God's standards. *Thus, a diligent
reliance upon the Greek text makes for the more accurate
exposition of the Word.*

Take the problem in the English translation of Galatians
1:16. Do the words, "to reveal his Son in me," mean that
God called Paul so that He could reveal the Lord Jesus to
Paul or to reveal Him through Paul to others? The Greek
word translated "reveal" answers the question at once. It is
the word ἀποκαλύπτω, which refers to the disclosure of
something by the removal of that which hitherto concealed
it, and refers especially to a subjective revelation to an
individual. A public disclosure of the Lord Jesus through
Paul would necessitate the fact that He had been previously
hidden from public knowledge, which is not the case,

since He had already been preached in the world. But He
had been previously hidden from Paul, which points to a
subjective revelation of the Lord Jesus to Paul within
Paul. This agrees with the context which has to do, not
with how Paul *preached* the gospel, but how he *received*
it. *Thus a problem which the English translation could
not settle is solved quickly by the Greek text. All of which
means that a study of the Greek text saves much of the
pastor's time and energy. And yet one of the usual excuses
for not using one's Greek is that we do not have the time.
Questions that are answered in hours of wading through
commentaries, can often be answered in five minutes by
recourse to a Greek lexicon.*

See what rich material one can get by squeezing a Greek
word, and squeezing it again, and again, and again. The
pastor is preaching on "The Rapture of the Church"
(1 Thess. 4:13-18). He is consulting his Greek text on the
word translated "caught up." It is ἁρπάζω. He finds that
the word means "to carry off by force." "That means," he
says, "that Satan will offer opposition to the passage of the
church through his realm in the atmosphere of this earth.
His demons will attempt to keep the church from going to
heaven. That means, that it will require the operation of
God's power to overcome the opposition of the demons
and take the church to heaven." He consults the lexicon
again, and finds the verb means "to claim for one's self
eagerly." That reminds him of the great Bridegroom, the
Lord Jesus, who will claim His Bride the church, eagerly.
Again he consults the lexicon, which is another way of
saying that he squeezes the Greek word. He finds that the
word was used proverbially with the meaning "to rescue
from the danger of destruction." "That means," he reflects,
"that the church will not go through the Great Tribulation. It will be snatched away before it begins." He squeezes
the word again. He finds that it means "to snatch out or

away," and he comes to the conclusion that the Rapture will be sudden, so sudden that it will catch both Satan and the Church by surprise, and so swift, that it will all be over before we know it. To wax facetious—we will go up so fast that there will hardly be time for the Calvinists to say to the Arminians, "I told you so." He squeezes the word again, and finds that it is used of divine power transferring a person marvellously and swiftly from one place to another. He reflects, "one minute on earth, the next minute in Glory."

Now, the point is, that none of these precious truths could he have gotten out of the words "caught up." He may have gotten them by a few hours searching through commentaries, that is, if the commentator was a close student of the Greek text. But, it took him not over ten minutes to check this word in a Greek lexicon, and write down his conclusions. Furthermore, he has taken this truth right from the Greek New Testament, and it has all the freshness of the original still upon it when he brings it to his people on the Lord's Day.

Then he looks up the word for air, ἀήρ, and the lexicon informs him that the Greeks had two words for air, ἀήρ, the lower, denser atmosphere, and αἰθήρ the upper, rarefied atmosphere. Paul uses the former here. The pastor reflects that the Greeks knew nothing of the stratosphere. Their purer, rarefied atmosphere started at the mountaintops. The pastor, a believer in verbal inspiration, says to himself, "The Holy Spirit led Paul to choose ἀήρ, not αἰθήρ, which means that the Lord Jesus will descend into the atmosphere surrounding this earth to a point below the mountaintops, and that is pretty close to this earth." Again, the point is, that the expositor who limits himself to the English translation, would never find this wonderful truth. But the student of the Greek New Testament always has fresh, new, precious truth like this at his disposal, to provide a spiritual banquet for the saints.

There is another valuable use to which word studies can be put. Sometimes, in order for an expositor to interpret properly a word in a certain context, he must see that word in a wide perspective. That is, he must trace the history of that word through all its usages in order to see it in a full-orbed and complete view. Take the problem of baptism in Romans 6:3-4. Because the word "baptize" usually has reference to the ceremony of water baptism, the English expositor will often interpret this passage as referring to water baptism. He never stops to think that the word is not native to the English language, and therefore has no meaning of its own; and, when appearing in the translation of the New Testament, the only legitimate meaning it can rightly have is that meaning which the word in the Greek text has. He does not reflect that the word is not a translation but a transliteration of the Greek word. Nor does he come to the conclusion that, in some contexts, βαπτίζω should be translated and in other places, transliterated.

But the expositor who uses his Greek says, "I must make a study of this word in its usage in classical Greek, and in the LXX, the papyri, and the New Testament." And so, with the aid of various Greek authorities, he makes a study of the Greek word. When he has done this, and not until he has done this, is he equipped to really come to grips with the problem of whether Romans 6:3-4, speaks of water or Holy Spirit baptism. The student's notes, giving this wide perspective of βαπτίζω, would be as follows:

BAPTIZE, BAPTISM. These two words are not native to the English language. Therefore, they do not have any intrinsic meaning of their own. The only rightful meaning they can have is the one that is derived from the Greek word of which they are the spelling. The verb is βαπτίζω from which, with a slight change in spelling, we get our word "baptize." The noun is βάπτισμα and, taking off the last letter, we have "baptism."

We will study these words first in their classical usage. The word βαπτίζω is related to another Greek word βάπτω. The latter meant "to dip, dip under." It was used of the smith tempering the red-hot steel. It was used also in the sense of "to dip in dye, to color, to steep." It was used of the act of dyeing the hair, and of glazing earthen vessels. It was used as a proverb in the sense of "steeping someone in crimson," that is, giving him a bloody coxcomb. It meant also "to fill by dipping in, to draw." It was used of a ship that dipped, that is, sank. βαπτίζω, the related word, meant "to dip repeatedly." It was used of the act of sinking ships. It meant also "to bathe." It was used in the phrase, "soaked in wine," where the word "soaked" is the meaning of βαπτίζω. It is found in the phrase, "over head and ears in debt," where the words "over head and ears" are the graphic picture of what the word meant. The word here means, therefore, "completely submerged." Our present day English equivalent would be "sunk." A βάπτης is one who dips or dyes. A βάπτισις is a dipping, bathing, a washing, a drawing of water. A βάπτισμα is that which is dipped. A βαπτιστήριον is a bathing place, a swimming bath. A βαπτιστής is one that dips, a dyer. βαπτός means "dipped, dyed, bright colored, drawn like water."

Βαπτίζω is used in the ninth book of the *Odyssey*, where the hissing of the burning eye of the Cyclops is compared to the sound of water where a smith dips (βαπτίζω) a piece of iron, tempering it. In the *Battle of the Frogs and Mice*, it is said that a mouse thrust a frog with a reed, and the frog leaped over the water (βαπτίζω) dyeing it with his blood. Euripides uses the word of a ship which goes down in the water and does not come back to the surface. Lucian dreams that he has seen a huge bird shot with a mighty arrow, and as it flies high in the air, it dyes (βαπτίζω) the clouds with his blood. An ancient scholium to the Fifth Book of the *Iliad* makes a wounded soldier dye (βαπτίζω) the earth with his blood. In Xenophon's *Anabasis*, we have the instance where the Greek soldiers placed (βαπτίζω) the points of their spears in a bowl of blood.

We come now to the usage of these words in Koine Greek, giving examples from the papyri, the LXX, and the New Testament.

In secular documents of the Koine period, Moulton and Milligan report the following uses of βαπτίζω: "a *submerged* boat, ceremonial ablutions, a person *flooded* or *overwhelmed* in calamities." They say that the word was used in its metaphorical sense even among uneducated people. A biblical example of this use is found in our Lord's speaking of His Passion as a "baptism" (Mark 10:38). These scholars report the use of βάπτω as referring to fullers and dyers. The word is used of colored garments, and of wool to be dyed. The word βάπτισμα is found in a question regarding a new baptism someone is reported to be preaching. This use of this noun is peculiar to the New Testament, and to ecclesiastical writers.

In the LXX we have in Leviticus 4:6 the words, "And the priest shall dip (βάπτω) his finger in the blood, and sprinkle (προσραίνω) of the blood seven times before the Lord." Here the word βάπτω is found in juxtaposition to προσραίνω, a verb closely allied to προσραντίζω, βάπτω meaning "to dip," the latter verb "to sprinkle."

In the New Testament we have the rich man asking that Lazarus dip (βάπτω) his finger in water and cool his tongue (Luke 16:24). In Hebrews 9:10 βάπτισμα is translated "washings" and refers to the ceremonial ablutions of

Judaism. In Mark 7:4 βάπτισμα is used of the ceremonial washing of cups, pots, brazen vessels, and tables. βάπτισμα is used in Matthew 3:7, and βαπτίζω in Matthew 3:16, and 1 Corinthians 1:14, of the rite of water baptism. In Mark 10:38 our Lord speaks of His sufferings on the cross as the βάπτισμα with which He is to be βαπτίζω.

In those examples of the various uses of the words βάπτω and βαπτίζω, we discover three distinct usages, a *mechanical* one, a *ceremonial* one, and a *metaphorical* one.

The *mechanical* usage can be illustrated by the action of the smith dipping the hot iron in water, tempering it, or the dyer dipping the cloth in the dye for the purpose of dyeing it. These instances of the use of our Greek word, give us the following definition of the word in its mechanical usage. The word refers to the introduction or placing of a person or thing into a new environment or into union with something else so as to alter its relationship to its previous environment or condition. While the word, we found, had other mechanical uses, yet the one that predominated above the others was the above use. The purely mechanical usage of our word is seen in the following places: Matthew 3:11 (second occurrence); Mark 1:8 (second), Luke 3:7 (second), 16:24; John 1:33 (second), 13:26; Acts 1:5 (second), 11:16 (second); 1 Corinthians 12:13; Galatians 3:27; Ephesians 4:5; Colossians 2:12; Revelation 19:13.

Before listing the places where the word occurs in its ceremonial usage, we will trace the usage of βαπτίζω back to Levitical washings. In the LXX (Lev. 14:8, 9; 15:5, 6, 7, 8, 10, 11, 13, 16, 18, 21, 22, 27; 16:4, 24, 28; 17:15) the word "wash" is λούω. This Greek word is found in Acts 22:16 in connection with the word βαπτίζω in the expression, "Be baptized and wash away thy sins." According to Mark 7:4 "washing of cups" (βαπτίζω), Luke 11:38, and

Hebrews 9:10, where βαπτίζω is used, that word seems to have been the technical term at the time for these washings. Expressions like those in Isaiah 1:16, and the prophecies like those in Ezekiel 36:25, 37:23, and Zechariah 13:1 are connected with the Levitical washings. Those washings and the prophecies are connected with the purification that followed the act of expiation or cleansing from sin (Exod. 19:14; Lev. 13:14; Heb. 10:22, 23). Thus, that for which the word βαπτίζω stood was not unknown to the Jews. Whereas the ceremonial washings of Leviticus were performed by the person himself, with one exception, and that was where Moses in installing Aaron and his sons as priests, himself washed them (Lev. 8:6), John βαπτίζω his converts himself.

βαπτίζω in the ministry of our Lord and John was, like the theocratic washings and purifications, a symbol whose design was to point to the purging away of sin on whom the rite was performed (Matt. 3:6, John 3:22-25). John's baptism was in response to the repentance of the individual (Matt. 3:11). It was connected with his message of an atonement for sin that was to be offered in the future, and the necessity of faith in that atonement (Acts 19:4).

John's baptism had looked ahead to a coming Savior. Paul's baptism, or Christian baptism, now looks back to a Savior who has died and who has risen again (Acts 19:5). That the rite of water baptism is the outward testimony of the inward fact of a person's salvation, and that it follows his act of receiving Christ as Savior and is not a prerequisite to his receiving salvation, is seen in the use of the preposition εἰς in Matt. 3:11 where the translation should read, "I indeed baptize you with water because of repentance." While the act of Christian baptism is a testimony of a person that his sins have been washed away, it also pictures and symbolizes the fact of the believing sinner's identification with Christ in His death, burial, and resurrection (Rom. 6), for βαπτίζω means, "to dip, to immerse." It never means "to sprinkle." The Greeks had a word for "sprinkle," namely, ῥαντίζω. The two words, βαπτίζω and ῥαντίζω are used in juxtaposition in Leviticus 4:6.

The following are the places where βαπτίζω is used of the baptism administered by John the Baptist and by the disciples of our Lord under the dispensation of law. Matthew 3:6, 11:1 (first mention), 13, 14, 16; Mark 1:4, 5, 8 (first mention), 9; Luke 3:7, 12, 16 (first mention), 21; 7:29, 30; John 1:25, 26, 28, 31, 33 (first mention); 3:22, 23, 26; 4:1, 2; 10:40; Acts 1:5 (first mention); 11:16 (first mention); 19:4 (first mention). The noun βάπτισμα when it is used of the baptism in the dispensation of law is found in the following places: Matthew 3:7; 21:25; Mark 1:4; 11:30; Luke 3:3; 7:29; 20:4; Acts 1:22; 10:37; 13:24; 18:25; 19:3-4.

The word βαπτίζω is used of the ablutions of the Jews which were extra-biblical, and which were called "the traditions of the elders" (Matt. 15:2), in Mark 7:4; Luke 11:38. The noun βάπτισμα is used in connection with the same practices in Matthew 7:4; Mark 7:8. It is used of the Levitical ablutions in Hebrews 6:2; 9:10.

βαπτίζω is used of Christian baptism in Matthew 28:19; Acts 2:38, 41; 8:12, 13, 16, 36, 38; 9:18; 10:47, 48; 16:15, 33; 18:8; 19:5; 22:16; 1 Corinthians 1:13, 14, 15, 16, 17; 15:29. βάπτισμα is used in 1 Peter 3:21 of Christian baptism.

The metaphorical use of βαπτίζω we find in Matthew 20:22, 23; Mark 10:38, 39; Luke 12:50. A metaphor is the use of a word or phrase literally denoting one kind of object or idea in place of another by way of suggesting a likeness or analogy between them; for example, "the ship *plows* the sea." In the above passages, our Lord is speaking of His sufferings in connection with the cross. He speaks of them as a baptism. The words were uttered while He

was on His way to Jerusalem to be crucified. John the
Baptist had announced His coming and had baptized the
multitudes. Our Lord's disciples had been baptizing during
the three years of His ministry. The words βαπτίζω and
βάπτισμα which are used by Matthew, Mark and Luke,
had by that time become the technical and common Greek
words used to describe the rite administered by John and
our Lord's disciples. Our Lord used the rite of baptism as
a metaphor to speak of His coming sufferings. Just as a
convert is plunged into the baptismal waters, He was
about to be plunged into His sufferings. Just as the person
would be immersed in the water, so He would be overwhelmed by His sufferings. Just as the person would come
up out of the water, so He would be freed from His
sufferings and arise from the dead.

There is one passage in which βαπτίζω is found that I
have not classified. It is 1 Corinthians 10:2, "were all
baptized unto Moses." Expositor's *Greek Testament* has
an illuminating note on it. "The 'cloud' shading and
guiding the Israelites from above, and the 'sea' making a
path for them through the midst and drowning their
enemies behind them, were glorious signs to 'our fathers'
of God's salvation; together they formed a washing of
regeneration (Titus 3:5), inaugurating the national life; as
it trode the miraculous path between upper and nether
waters, Israel was born into its divine estate. Thus 'they all
received their baptism *unto Moses* in the cloud and in the
sea' since in this act they committed themselves to the
guidance of Moses, entering through him into acknowledged fellowship with God."

After making a thorough study of βαπτίζω, the student
is ready to come to grips with the problem of baptism in
Romans 6:3-4. He has found that the word has a metaphorical, ceremonial, and a mechanical usage. He argues

that its use in this place is certainly not metaphorical. Nor can it be ceremonial, since that which is accomplished by the baptism here is the breaking of the power of indwelling sin (v. 2), and the impartation of the divine nature (v. 4). Since both of those require the exertion of supernatural power, the baptism here must be supernatural in its character; therefore, mechanical, not ceremonial. Recalling his definition of the mechanical usage of βαπτίζω as "the introduction or placing of a person or thing into a new environment or into union with something else so as to alter its condition or its relationship to its previous environment or condition," he appends the following note to his findings, which gives the conclusion to which he has come regarding the kind of baptism spoken of in Romans 6:3-4. Observe how perfectly this meaning is in accord with the usage of the word in Romans 6:3-4, where the believing sinner is baptized into vital union with Jesus Christ. The believing sinner is introduced or placed in Christ, thus coming into union with Him. By that action he is taken out of his old environment and condition in which he had lived, the First Adam, and is placed into a new environment and condition, the Last Adam. By this action his condition is changed from that of a lost sinner with a totally depraved nature to that of a saint with a divine nature. His relationship to the law of God is changed from that of a guilty sinner to that of a justified saint. All this is accomplished by the act of the Holy Spirit introducing or placing him into vital union with Jesus Christ. No ceremony of water baptism ever did that. The entire context is supernatural in its character. The Greek word here should not be transliterated but translated, and the translation should read: "As many as were introduced (placed) into Christ Jesus, into His death were introduced. Therefore we

were buried with Him through the aforementioned introduction into His death." The same holds true of 1 Corinthians 12:13 which should be translated, "For through
the instrumentality of one Spirit were we all placed into
one body." It is because we so often associate the English
word "baptism" with the rite of water baptism that we
read that ceremony into Romans 6. A student from Greece
in one of the writer's Greek classes, who learned to speak
that language as his mother tongue and studied it in
the schools of Greece, stated during a class discussion that
the Greek reader would react to the Greek text of Romans
and the word βαπτίζω as the writer has.

1. *Vocabulary of the Greek Testament*, Moulton and Milligan.

7
The Practical Use of the Fuller or Expanded Translation

B Y A FULLER or expanded translation is meant a rendering of the Greek text that brings over into the English, much of the richness that is left in the original by the standard translations because these latter are held down to a minimum of words. This is done by using as many English words as are needed to bring out the details in the Greek text.

For instance, take the fuller or expanded translation of John 15:7. *If ye make your home in Me, and my words make their home in you, whatever your heart desires, I command you to ask, at once, something for yourself, and it shall become yours.* Compare this for richness of content, and for detail and clarity, with the standard translation which you are using. Your translation is correct, but it does not bring out all the richness and detail of the original.

In producing this expanded translation, the following work had to be done. Thayer was consulted on the verb μένω. A study of the usage of this verb in the New Testament, was made with the help of Englishman's Greek Concordance. The word "will" opened up the study of the synonyms θέλω and βούλομαι, the former referring to a desire which comes from the emotions, the latter, to one that comes from the reason. The verb "ask" was found to be in the imperative mood, which mood issues a command; in the aorist tense, which tense when used in the imperative mood makes the command one to be obeyed at once; and in the indirect middle voice, which speaks of the subject acting in his own interest, thus asking for himself. The verb itself meant "to ask for something to be given." The word "done" is the translation of γίνομαι which means "to become."

Now, this is translation, not paraphrase. It is not even what might be called a free translation. It holds rigidly except in one place to the actual meaning of the Greek words. That exception is where we have tried to indicate a desire which came from the emotions by using the word "heart," which does not appear in the text.

When this Scripture was read from the Greek New Testament in a Greek church in the first century, the audience got what we have put in our expanded translation, since a Greek, for instance, would take notice of the tense, mood, and voice of the verb, and in the twinkling of an eye put together those three thoughts indicated above. He would also distinguish between the synonyms. Thus, the first century audience, listening to the reading of the Greek scriptures, would get far more from that reading than the present day church audience when listening to the reading of the English Bible. That brings us to the question, *why deprive a present-day audience of that added richness and detail which the standard translations do not bring out, when the pastor, trained to work in the Greek New Testament, is able to bring it to his audience?*

Would not the expanded translation of this verse make a splendid basis for a brief message on prayer just before the saints engage in the priestly ministry of intercession on prayer-meeting night? What is to hinder the pastor from using it? He need not bring it in written form to the desk from which he speaks. He should know it so well that, as he takes up the word studies one by one, he can build his expanded translation as he goes through the verse. The saints, of course, are made to understand that the pastor is not offering any corrections on the standard translation being used, but only bringing out some of the richness left behind in the Greek text. Such a translation the saints will roll over their spiritual tongues for the rest of the week, to the delight of their spiritual gustatory nerves, the enrichment of their knowledge of the Word, and the strengthening of their prayer-lives.

Or, take the fuller translation of *1 Peter 2:11, 12,* as an example of the added richness of detail which can be brought to an audience. *Divinely loved ones, I beg of you, please, as those who are sojourning alongside of a foreign population (should), be constantly holding yourselves back from the fleshly cravings, cravings of such a nature that, like an army carrying on a military campaign, they are waging war, hurling themselves down upon your soul; holding your manner of life among the unsaved steadily beautiful in its goodness, in order than in the thing in which they defame you as those who do evil (namely, in your Christianity), because of your works beautiful in their goodness which they are constantly, carefully, and attentively watching, they may glorify God in the day of His overseeing care.* Compare this with your standard translation. The pastor is speaking, for instance, to his young people on the subject, "The Deportment of the Christian Among the Unsaved." The young people know that their pastor is a deep student of the Word, and that he uses his Greek. The freshness and the graphic qualities of the translation will command their careful attention to the Word. Sometimes the beautiful, measured diction of the King James Version dulls the spiritual ear of the listener by reason of his familiarity with it, and when an expositor uses a fresh translation, the attention is at once awakened. See how much more that pastor can bring to his listeners from an expanded translation like this.

The work of producing such a translation is taxing, and arduous, and exhausting. But it is not difficult if one knows his Greek and is the recipient of the teaching ministry of the Holy Spirit. This latter makes all the difference in the world. That which, without this ministry, would have been a most unpleasant and difficult task for the pastor, becomes with it, a most delightful and easy occupation. Where the pastor is fully yielded to the Spirit so that He might glorify the Lord Jesus in his study and expositon of the Word, such deficiencies as a lack of a brilliant mind and an unusual expertness in handling the Greek text, are counter-balanced by the illumination afforded by the Spirit. The Holy Spirit can give one a pair of Greek eyes to see, a Greek mind to think, and a Greek tongue to expound the wonders of truth in the Greek text. The riches of the Greek New Testament are not reserved only for the pastor who has a brilliant mind and scholarly gifts. The Holy Spirit, the Great Interpreter, is able to make these available to the average Greek student of the Word.

See the flood of light thrown upon the English translation you are using by this fuller translation of 1 Peter 1:22. *Wherefore, having purified your souls by means of your obedience to the truth, resulting in not an assumed but a genuine affection and fondness for the brethren, an affection and fondness that springs from your hearts by reason of the pleasure you take in them; from the heart love each other with an intense reciprocal love that springs from your hearts because of your estimation of the preciousness of the brethren, and which is divinely self-sacrificial in its essence.* At once the subject of the message literally leaps at one from the Greek text, "Amalgamated Love." Take the difficult *Kenosis* passage of *Philippians 2:5-8.* Compare the following translation with the standard translation you are using, and see how much clearer it is. *This mind be constantly having in you which was also in Christ Jesus, who has always been and at present continues to subsist in that mode of being in which He gives outward expression of His essential nature, that of Deity, an expression that comes from and is truly representative of His intrinsic nature, and who did not after weighing the facts, consider it a treasure to be clutched and retained at all hazards, to be equal with Deity (in the expression of the divine essence), but emptied Himself, having taken the outward expression of a bondslave, which expression came from and was truly representative of His inward nature, entering into a new state of existence, that of mankind. And being found in outward guise as man, He stooped very low, having become obedient to the extent of death, even such a death as that upon a cross.* After the pastor has worked out a translation such as this, he is ready to come to grips with the exegesis of this profound portion of Scripture. When he does this kind of work, he is forced to think things through. He will not content himself with a surface interpretation, repeating words and phrases the meaning of which he has only a superficial understanding. He will strike rock bottom in his interpretation, so far as it is humanly possible to do so, and his exegesis will be built on a solid foundation.

When the pastor puts himself to the task of doing translation work in preparation for his messages, he will find that he will not necessarily use the entire translation as such. But brief snatches of it will creep out in his sermon, bringing with them all the force, freshness, and clarity of the Greek text. For instance, instead of the words, *Whom resist steadfast in the faith* (1 Peter 5:9), he will find himself saying, *Stand immovable against his onset, solid as a rock in your faith,* which is a great deal stronger.

Suppose the pastor is preaching an expository sermon on the subject, "A Portrait of the Suffering Servant of Jehovah," and that his expository unit is 1 Peter 2:18-25. After having made a detailed study of the Greek text, he makes this translation. (18) *Household slaves, put yourselves in constant subjection with every fear to your absolute lords and masters; not only to those who are good at heart, but also to those who are against you: (19) for this subjection to those who are against you is something which is beyond the ordinary course of what might be expected, and is therefore commendable, namely, when a person because of the conscious sense of his relation to God bears up under pain, suffering unjustly. (20) For what sort of fame is it when you fall short of the mark and are pummeled with the fist, you endure this patiently? But if when you are in the habit of doing good and then suffer constantly for it, and this you patiently endure, this is an unusual and not-to-be-expected action, and therefore commendable in the sight of God. (21) For to this very thing were you called (namely, to patient endurance in the case of unjust punishment), because Christ also suffered on your behalf, leaving behind for you a model to imitate, in order that by close application you might follow in His footprints; (22) who never in a single instance committed a sin, and in whose mouth, after careful scrutiny, there was found not even craftiness; (23) who, when His heart was being wounded with an accursed sting, and when He was being made the object of harsh rebuke and biting, never retaliated, and who, while suffering, never threatened, but rather kept on delivering all into the keeping of the One who judges righteously; (24) who Himself carried up to the cross our sins in His own body and offered Himself there as on an altar, doing this in order that we, having died with respect to sin, might live with respect to righteousness, by means of whose bleeding stripes you were healed. (25) For you were straying like sheep, but you have turned back to the Shepherd and overseer of your souls.*

What a grasp he now has of that portion of God's Word. What a vivid picture of the Lord Jesus he has. The New Testament is filled with portraits of the Son of God, painted by the brush of the Holy Spirit, every stroke of the brush, a Greek word. In an art gallery, a copy of an original painting is never as good as the masterpiece which the artist painted. The lights and shadows are never as clearly marked, the colors never so vivid. It is so with respect to the English New Testament. The portraits of the Lord Jesus are true copies of those in the Greek, but they are never so vivid and clear. The expanded translation we have offered brings out more of the vividness and detail, but even that is not the same as the original painted by the Holy Spirit. The pastor who uses his Greek New Testament has access to the original portraits of the Lord Jesus painted by the Holy Spirit. He can therefore bring a clearer picture of Him to his hearers. He comes to know Him better himself, and thus comes to be more like Him. Even Erasmus, the great humanist, could say in the preface of his Greek Testament; "These holy pages will summon up the living image of His mind. They will give you Christ Himself, talking, healing, dying, rising, the whole Christ in a word; they will give Him to you in an intimacy so close that He would be less visible to you if He stood before your eyes." What that great scholar saw only dimly, yet with great appreciation, the humble pastor filled with the Holy Spirit can see in his Greek New Testament with all the vividness, beauty, and life which only the Holy Spirit can shed upon the page of Holy Writ.

One of the most heart-breaking and deplorable things in the 2000 years of church history, is the almost universal neglect by preachers, of the Greek New Testament, with the consequent impoverishment of its message. What a wealth of truth the church has missed in all these years, hidden away back there in the Greek text. Only the one who has fallen in love with the Greek New Testament, only the one who has tasted of its riches, can appreciate the loss involved in its neglect. As the apostasy grows, and the darkness of this age grows deeper, it behooves those servants of God who have a knowledge of Greek, to make the best use of their Greek New Testaments. Thus, the light of the gospel will become more intense and will pierce the surrounding darkness with a brighter beam, lighting many a ship-wrecked sailor on the vast ocean of human life, to the haven of rest, even the Lord Jesus. The Greek New Testament blazed the way for the Reformation, and pierced the spiritual darkness of the middle ages, lighting up the whole of Europe. The Word of God will glow with a great brilliance in the pulpit of any pastor who is a student of that Book of books.

8

The Practical Method of Mastering the Greek Text in Preparation for Expository Preaching

U P TO THIS point in our discussion of the practical use of the Greek New Testament, we have considered one way of using the Greek text. The pastor in his sermon preparation, uses the English translation in his study, and supplements it with help from the Greek New Testament in the strategic and difficult places. This method is a concession to circumstances. The pastor may have excellent pastoral gifts, but does not have exceptional ability as a student. Or, he may not have had enough training to be able to do more than this with his Greek. Or, he may be in a position where the necessity of earning his living encroaches upon his study time. Or, he may not be in robust health so that he can spend time and energy in arduous, exhaustive study. But, even such a method will bring large results over and above those that he would have had, had he confined himself to the English New Testament. And we have nothing to say against such a procedure. All honor to the man who endeavors to enrich his ministry

115

and make his Bible exposition more accurate even by this method.

There is, however, another way, and that is by working from the Greek text itself. This chapter will be devoted to the presentation of a practical method of doing research work in the Greek text in preparation for teaching or preaching.

In addition to his sermon preparation, a pastor should be constantly working in some New Testament book, using the method about to be described. He should set aside a certain number of hours a week for this study, and hold himself rigidly to it. This will result in certain benefits in his life and ministry. In the first place, it will help him to keep up his study habits, learned and practiced while in school. *The man who starts to coast on what he knows, is on the toboggan.* Sooner or later his sermon barrel will be empty, and he will have nothing with which to replenish it. But let him work in the Greek New Testament a certain number of hours a week, and he will always have rich, fresh, and new material, and a thousand and one suggestions for new sermons presented in a new way. Sermon texts and subjects will literally jump out of the Greek text before his eyes. He will have more material at his disposal than he has time to preach.

In the second place, after he has worked through a Bible book, he has detailed exegetical notes on every Greek word in that book. He can now deliver a series of expository messages which will carry him through the book, teach the book in a week-day Bible class, or use it for brief spiritual talks on prayer-meeting nights. Since he has already done the research work and has it on his finger-tips, so to speak, he does not need to spend so much time in preparation for his message. This should prove a boon to the busy pastor where a particular week may be crowded with sick-calls, weddings, or funerals. All he does is to sit down with his English Bible, his Greek text, and his notes before him, and he has everything at his disposal that he needs. In his sermon preparation aside from the preparation he makes in the study of a Bible book, the pastor should do the same intensive research work in the expository unit he is to present. Should circumstances arise which make this impossible, he can at least use the method presented in previous chapters in this book. We will now consider the practical method which a pastor should use in mastering the Greek text of a Bible book.

For a short, simple, and rich book let him start with Paul's letter to the Philippians. Suppose that he has four word sudies in his library, *Expositor's Greek Testament* (X), *Vincent's Word Studies* (V), *Bishop Lightfoot on Philippians* (L), *Alford's Greek Testament* (A). He will have those open at the place where the Philippian epistle is treated. He will have his lexicons ready, *Thayer* (Th), *Cremer* (C), *Moulton and Milligan* (M. & M.), *Bagster* (B), *Englishman's Greek Concordance* (E), and his grammars, *Davis* (D) and *Dana and Mantey* (D. & M.). He will provide himself with several blocks of 8½ x 5½ unlined white paper. He will record his notes on the length of the paper, placing chapter and verse treated in the upper right-hand corner, and the page number in the upper left-hand corner.

He will put down the first Greek word in the verse, consult each of his authorities on the word, put down what he will need to enable him to present the truth contained clearly to his people, and after each note, he will list the authority from which he took the material, using the initial letter in a parenthesis or a circle. These notes need not be in the words of the Greek authority necessarily, preferably in his own words. He will first of all put down the tense, mood, and voice of the verbs, the gender, number, and case of the nouns, or any other item of grammar or syntax that has to do with the word. In other words, he will treat the word grammatically and also with respect to its syntax. Upon the basis of this grammar or syntax, he will often make some interpretation rich in content and accurate in meaning. When he comes to make his translation of the verse, these points in grammar and syntax will also be needed. After he has done that, he should list the comments, interpretations, and translation material which the lexicons and word studies give him. In the case where these authorities duplicate each other, it is enough to make the one note and list the various authorities after it. The reason why it is a good practice to list authorities, is that when there is a divergence of opinion, one can weigh the evidence on each side and come to a conclusion that is based upon the majority opinion, or upon any one of the authorities, and his reasons for presenting the interpretation he gives. Sometimes the pastor will have enough confidence in one authority, to take *his* conclusions as against those of the others. There is another advantage in quoting authorities. After one comes back to his notes, he may not understand something he has written, owing to the fact that the note is too brief. If he has the authority, he can quickly turn back to it for more details.

After the pastor has made a study of each word in a verse, he is ready to translate it. The reason why he should make a translation is that it forces him to come to grips with the exact meaning of the verse. His translation may be a bit cumbersome, and not so polished as the King James Version. But it should have more detail in it, and in some instances, it should be clearer to him than that translation, and for the reason that he uses more English words. There should be more in it than in the translation he is using. He is not going to read his translation to his audience nor have it published. His purpose in making the translation is that he might obtain a clearer understanding of the verse and thus be able to explain it in a simpler way to his people.

When he has finished one verse in this way, he should go to the next, and in that way work through the entire book. This is laborious, taxing, exhausting, patient, and slow work. But nothing of any real merit is ever produced except by good hard work. The pastor will find that it is well worth the effort. As he does the work, he will be picking up golden nuggets of truth that will enrich his own life, and provide sermon and teaching material and subjects which he can use even before he actually presents the book in a series of expository messages or teaches it in a Bible class. So much for the method. Now, for a sample of what the pastor's notes should look like.

PAGE ONE.   *Philippians*   1:1
Παῦλος; masculine, singular, nominative case, proper noun.
1. The Greek transliteration of a Latin name *Paulus*. His other name was Σαῦλος (Th.).
2. Deissmann has shown that the apostle was already in possession of the double name at the time referred to in Acts 13:9 (M.&M.).
3. *Paulus* means *little*. According to some, both names were borne by Paul in his childhood, *Paulus* being the one by which he was known among the Gentiles, and which was subsequently assumed by him to the exclusion of the other, in order to indicate his position as the friend and teacher of the Gentiles. The practice of adopting Gentile names may be traced through all periods of Hebrew history. (V)

4. The Hebrew name Σαῦλος means "asked for" (Th.). The word means also "to pray."

5. Some think that the name *Paulus* was an allusion to his diminutive stature (V). Surely, he exemplified in his life of prayer, that for which his Hebrew name stood.

6. The omission of Paul's official title ἀπόστολος may be accounted for by the general, unofficial, personal, affectionate character of the letter (V).

Τιμόθεος, masculine, singular, nominative case, proper noun.

1. From τιμάω "to honor," and θεός "God," thus, one who honors God. Possibly indicative of the character of Timothy, since he had a godly grandmother who nurtured him in the faith. His father was a Greek, his mother a Jewess, the name given him as a boy, in the hope of his exemplifying its meaning in later life.

2. The only significance belonging to the mention of Timothy was that he was a well-known person at Philippi, that the Philippians owed him much, and that he was to visit them again. The Philippian letter claims to be Paul's alone. Paul uses the first person singular in v. 3. (X) (A).

δοῦλοι, masculine, plural, nominative case.

1. Derived by most from δέω to tie, bind (Th.). Thus, one bound to another as a slave. A man of servile condition, a bondman, one who gives himself up wholly to another's will or dominion, one devoted to another to the disregard of one's own interests (Th.).

2. Liddell and Scott (classical), a slave, strictly one born so, opposed to ἀνδράποδον, a person kidnapped or taken in war and made a slave.

3. *Moulton and Milligan* on δοῦλος refer to Deissmann's *Light from the Ancient East* on use of word.

Deissmann says that the use of *servant* as a translation for δοῦλος totally effaces the ancient significance of the Greek word. He speaks of the metaphor Paul uses of our redemption from the slavery to sin, a metaphor influenced by the customs and technical formulae of sacred manumissions in antiquity. The custom by which the manumission of a slave took place, was for the owner of the slave to come with him to the temple of the pagan god, sell him to the god, and receive the purchase money from the temple treasury, the slave having previously paid it in there out of his savings. The slave is now the property of the god, not a slave, however, but a protégé of the god. So far as the rest of the world is concerned, including his former master, he is a free man. At the utmost, a few pious obligations to his old master are imposed upon him. Paul is referring in the expression δοῦλοι Χριστοῦ ᾽Ιησοῦ to the fact that he was a slave of sin, and that he has been liberated by Christ Jesus through the purchase price, His precious blood.

4. Deissmann refers to the fact that there were particular individuals who had the honor of being designated as "Slaves of the Emperor" in the Imperial Cult of the Caesar. Paul, by the use of δοῦλος, speaks of the honor of being an imperial slave of the King of kings, the Lord Jesus.

5. M. and M. speak of the growing tendency in the LXX of emphasizing the distance between God and man by the use of δοῦλος which speaks of a slave in a most servile condition.

6. δοῦλος, already used in the LXX in a distinctly religious sense, is used by Paul here to express intense fervor of devotion, and to include the idea of a special calling and function in Christ's kingdom, parallel in its application in the Old Testament to the prophets.

There is also genuine humility in the contrast between δοῦλος and ἅγιος. Paul only calls himself ἀπόστολος when he is in a commanding mood (X).

Χριστοῦ 'Ιησοῦ masculine, singular, genitive case, genitive of possession (D.&M.). Paul is proud of the fact that the Lord Jesus owns him.

1. Χριστός, from χρίω *to anoint*, thus the Anointed One.

It is added as an appellative ('Messiah,' 'anointed') to the proper name 'Ιησοῦς (Th).

2. 'Ιησοῦς, a transliteration of the Hebrew word *Jehoshua* meaning "Jehovah saves."

3. The order of the names strikes the keynote of Paul's attitude towards his Master. He delights to think of Him in royal dignity, the Messiah who was once Jesus, being now Κύριος (X).

πᾶσιν τοῖς ἁγίοις, masculine, plural, dative.

1. πᾶς appears often in the opening verses to show Paul's strict impartiality, perhaps in view of some pretensions to superiority which appeared in the Philippian church (X) (A).

2. In Paul's personal addresses in this epistle, the word *all* occurs nine times. It is sufficiently accounted for by the expansiveness of grateful Christian feeling which marks the entire letter, and it is doubtful whether it has any definite or conscious connection with the social rivalries hinted at in this epistle (V).

3. By the use of πᾶς, Paul wishes to put those Philippians who had not sent to his support, on a level in his affection with those who had (A).

4. ἁγίοις speaks of the idea of consecration to God, and suggests also in every New Testament instance that side of the Christian life which stands in most glaring contrast with the impurity and sensuality of the Gentiles, holiness of heart and conduct (X).

5. ἁγίοις is to be taken as a noun, not as an adjective. The word is taken from the Old Testament. The Israelites were ἅγιοι, holy, separated, and consecrated (V) (L).

6. ἁγίζω in classical Greek meant "to set apart for the gods." The word in the New Testament is ἁγιάζω which means "to set apart for God" (C). Thus, the ἅγιοι at Philippi were those who were set apart in Christ Jesus for God. The necessity for a separated life is seen in the meaning of the word. Those who are set apart for God *positionally* should live separated lives *experimentally*.

ἐν Χριστῷ 'Ιησοῦ, locative of sphere.

1. The locative of sphere confines one idea within the bounds of another (D&M). The idea in ἁγίοις, namely, the fact that believers in Philippi are separated ones, is confined in the words "Christ Jesus." This distinguishes them from the ἅγιοι of the pagan religions and temples. Their separation is in Christ Jesus in that they are positionally in Him and vitally joined to Him. Their separation is circumscribed by Christ Jesus, limited to and conditioned by Christ Jesus.

2. The gist of this formula ἐν Χριστῷ is nothing else than Paul's mystic faith, in which the believer gives up himself, his own life, to Christ, and possesses the life of Christ in himself: he in Christ, and Christ in him; he dead with Christ, and Christ become his life (X).

ἐπισκόποις, masculine, plural, dative case, from ἐπισκέπτομαι which means "to look upon or after, to look upon in order to help or benefit, to look after, have a care for, provide for" (Th). An ἐπίσκοπος is one therefore who performs these duties.

1. In the LXX, almost always an official in charge of work being done on repairs in the Temple, in the

rebuilding of Jerusalem, or is used of an officer in the army. In New Testament is often the same person as the πρεσβύτερος (overseers) (Acts 20:28) who is concerned with shepherding the flock of God. The strong tradition of early Church confirms this. πρεσβύτερος is the title, ἐπίσκοπος the function of the church official (X).

2. The translation of the word should be "overseers." In the apostolic writings, it is synonymous with presbyter or elder (V).

3. The contributions sent to Paul by the Philippian church were probably sent in the name of the officers as well as of the church generally. It seems hardly probable that this mention was intended, as some have thought, to strengthen the hands of the presbyters and deacons, their authority being endangered. The dissensions in the Philippian Church do not appear to have touched the officers (L).

4. There was usually one church in each city with several bishops or elders.

5. The word is descriptive of function, not office, "with them that have oversight" (M&M).

6. The word was used as an official title in pre-Christian times, for instance, an ἐπίσκοπος was amongst the officials of the temple of Apollo. It was used of supervisors (M&M).

διακόνοις, masculine, plural, dative.

1. Of uncertain origin, but by no means, as was formerly thought compounded of διά and κόνις, so as to mean "raising dust by hastening." Buttmann thinks it is derived from obsolete διάκω allied with διώκω

"to pursue." It refers to one who executes the commands of another, especially of a master; an attendant, a servant, one who ministers (Th).

2. Trench says that it represents the servant in his activity.

3. A deacon, one who by virtue of his office assigned him by the church, cares for the poor and has charge of and distributes the money collected for their use (Th).

4. Expositor's speaks of the clear distinction in 1 Timothy 3, which is drawn between the διάκονος and the ἐπίσκοπος. In the early Christian church the most necessary Christian *service* would be the care of the sick and poor. So the deacon must neither be double-tongued nor "a lover of dirty gain," for in his work of visiting, he would have temptations to gossip and slander on the one hand, and to picking and stealing from the alms on the other. It seems natural that these officers should be mentioned, since the Philippian epistle was a "thank-you letter" for the gift, the management of which would be in the hands of the controlling authorities in the church (X).

5. The origin of the office is found in Acts 6:1-6. The work of the deacons was, primarily, the relief of the sick and poor. But spiritual ministrations naturally developed in connection with their office. Ignatius says of deacons, "They are not ministers of food and drink, but *servants* of the Church of God. Let all pay respect to the deacons as to Jesus Christ. Respect the deacons as the voice of God enjoins you." In "The Teaching of the Twelve Apostles," the local churches

or individual congregations are ruled by bishops and deacons (V).

6. The simple juxtaposition of the officers with the members of the church, and indeed their being placed *after* those members, shows the absence of hierarchical views such as those in the Epistles of the apostolic fathers (A).

TRANSLATION. *Paul and Timothy, bondservants of Christ Jesus, to all the separated and consecrated ones in Christ Jesus, those in Philippi, with the overseers and deacons.*

The habit of explaining the Word through the use of word studies, results in the enrichment of the message by the addition of many details which the English translation does not bring out. Helpful, delightful, fresh, and practical applications of truth to the Christian life can be brought out from Τιμόθεος, δοῦλος, ἅγιος. Valuable instruction regarding church officers and their duties comes from ἐπίσκοπος and διάκονος. Truth regarding the person and work of the Lord Jesus can be brought out in the study of Χριστός and ᾽Ιησοῦς. The way therefore to get rich truth is to study *words*, the *words* in the Greek text. This form of presentation is at once simple and delightful. The saints will revel in it.

After the pastor has treated the Greek text of Philippians in the detailed and intensive way suggested above, he can supplement his work with the reading of several good books on Paul's letter, and then he is ready to preach a series of expository sermons from the epistle, teach it in a week-day Bible class, or use it for simple, brief messages on prayer-meeting nights.

9

The Practical Greek Student's Kit of Tools

G OLDEN NUGGETS of truth do not lie on the surface, even of the Greek text of the New Testament. They are embedded deep within the intricate formations of gender, number, and case, of tense, mood, and voice, of prepositions, synonyms, and word studies. The student needs a good kit of Greek tools with which to extract them. There is a tool for every purpose. Or, it may take a combination of several different tools to dig down and bring up a golden boulder rather than a nugget once in awhile. The student must know his tools, and how to use them. The purpose of this chapter is to introduce the student to a practical, simple, and effective kit of tools.

It is assumed that the Greek student has a good grammar dealing with the elements of Greek. One that presents eight cases in Greek rather than five, is to be preferred, since it more sharply defines the delicate distinctions between some of the cases. *Case is not a matter of form, but*

128 The Practical Use of the Greek New Testament

of function. For instance, although the genitive and the ablative cases have the same case ending, yet they have quite different functions. The genitive is the *specifying* case, the ablative, the *whence* case. The former describes, whereas the latter shows source, and speaks of separation. While the case ending of the locative, instrumental, and dative cases is the same, yet the locative is the case of *location*, specifying the location within which the action of the verb takes place, the instrumental is the case of *means* or *association*, designating the instrument by which the action of the verb is accomplished, and the dative is the case of *personal interest*, designating the person or thing in whose interest the action of the verb is performed. Excellent grammars that present the eight cases are *Beginner's Grammar of the Greek New Testament* by William Hersey Davis and *Essentials of New Testament Greek* by Ray Summers. If the student has been out of school for some years, and has not kept up his Greek, he will need such a grammar in order to brush up on his declensions and conjugations.

The second tool he will need is *A Manual Grammar of the Greek New Testament*, by H. E. Dana and Julius R. Mantey, MacMillan, New York. Whether he has had a course in syntax or not, this book is most highly recommended because of the simplicity and clarity of its presentation. This is a *must* in the Greek student's kit of tools. The writer has found it invaluable in his exegetical work in the Greek New Testament. It gives definitions of the tenses and the cases, presenting classifications of each, so that when one comes to a knotty problem having to do with a tense or case, he can turn to the one in question, consult its various classifications, and usually find the very help he needs by which to solve the problem. The section on the use of the article is most illuminating. Many problems in exegesis are solved by a knowledge of the syntax of the article. The work of these scholars on prepositions is based upon a knowledge of their papyri usage. The preposition is treated under the following headings: its root meanings, its meanings in composition, its resultant meanings, and its remote meanings. Examples from the Greek New Testament are given so that when a student fails to understand the particular significance of a preposition in a certain context, he can consult their presentation of that preposition, and quickly find help. Conjunctions and particles are also treated in a thorough way. Infinitives come in for their share of thorough, plain, and simple treatment, as do the participles. Under the uses of the infinitive, the book presents the verbal uses and the substantival uses, the various classifications of these uses being illustrated by New Testament quotations. The work on the participles is most satisfying and helpful. It will be found useful in the solution of problems of interpretation arising from the use of the participle in the text. This book includes a treatment of the moods, and the *aktionsart* of the tenses within the moods. This grammar also has the advantage of having the eight cases. Should the student wish to continue his studies in syntax, the book he would want is *A Grammar of the Greek New Testament in the Light of Historical Research*, by A. T. Robertson, a volume of 1454 pages, a massive work, a monument and milestone representing the distinct advance in the knowledge of Koine Greek which this great scholar in a lifetime of prodigious labors, has offered to the world of New Testament research and scholarship. The publishers are George H. Doran Company, New York. A shorter grammar of the same type is *A Greek Grammar of the New Testament and Other Early Christian Literature* by F. Blass and A. Debrunner. It is published by the University of Chicago Press.

After grammars, we will list lexicons. For a general, all-round lexicon of the Greek New Testament, we would suggest Thayer's *Greek-English Lexicon of the New Testament*, publishers, The American Book Company, New York. Another lexicon is *A Greek-English Lexicon of the New Testament and Other Early Christian Literature* by William F. Arndt and F. Wilbur Gingrich. It is published by the University of Chicago Press. The latter lexicon has the advantage of the contemporary literature of the New Testament period which material was not available at the time of the compiling of Thayer's lexicon. The Thayer lexicon is based on the classical and New Testament uses of the words, but has the advantage of listing all the places in the Greek New Testament in which the word is used. Because Arndt and Gingrich is a lexicon of the entire period and not just the New Testament, it gives only a sampling of where the word is used in the secular and religious literature of the period. For a lexicon that specializes in the important Greek words dealing with doctrinal and theological subjects in the New Tesament, we would highly recommend *Biblico-Theological Lexicon of New Testament Greek* by Hermann Cremer. This scholar has given us a lexicon which treats the individual word in a far more detailed way than Thayer, tracing the history of the word sometimes from classical Greek, through the LXX and into the New Testament. He is sound in his doctrine and theology. This lexicon will not take the place of Thayer, since it treats only a limited number of words. It is published by Charles Scribner's Sons, New York. It is a monumental piece of work and should prove very helpful.

The student should also have a *Greek-English Lexicon* by Liddell and Scott. That will prove very useful in ascertaining the classical usage of the Greek word, and in the case of words that do not have a New Testament doctrinal or theological content of meaning, will be of help in interpreting the Greek New Testament. Under lexicons we would also list *A Vocabulary of the Greek Testament* by Moulton and Milligan. This is the last word in lexicons. It represents the latest and most advanced researches in the meanings of the words of the Greek New Testament. The work is based on the papyri. These scholars have assembled a great list of words found in the New Testament and also found in the papyri documents. They give illustrations of their use in these secular documents, and from these illustrations, the Greek student can make his own definitions. This is the final court of appeal when the expositor wants to know exactly how the Greek word was used by the people who spoke the *Koine*. One cannot recommend this work too highly for its up-to-date scholarship in the Greek New Testament field. The scientific approach to the problem of the exact meaning of a word, is the *historical-grammatical method*. The attempt is made to learn what the word meant to the people of the age when a document was written. When one gets the historical background of a word, its grammatical significance, and its syntactical relationship to the rest of the sentence in which it occurs, one is not apt to go wrong in arriving at its exact meaning and use. Right here this lexicon is of immense help. If the student would like to read the fascinating story of the discovery of the relationship that exists between the Greek of the New Testament and that of the contemporary secular documents known as the papyri, we would recommend *Light From the Ancient East* by Adolph Deissmann, the scholar who made the discovery. In this book, he deals with the Greek used in the writing of the New Testament, giving photographs of papyri manuscripts and furnishing also their translations. Those throw a flood of light upon the New Testament, and give one a first-hand picture of the people and how they lived and spoke in Gospel times. If one wants to broaden his view of New Testament Greek, here is a book that is an eye-opener.

There is one more lexicon that the average Greek student needs, and that is Bagster's *Analytical Greek Lexicon*. Its chief use is not in defining words, but in locating forms. Unless one keeps up with his declensions and conjugations, he becomes rusty. We would concede that the pastor is too busy and has more important work to do than to keep these fresh in his mind. Furthermore, there are some forms so far away from home that, unless one is thoroughly schooled in these irregular forms, he is at a loss to identify them. Here is where this lexicon comes in handy. It saves the busy pastor a great deal of time. He can very quickly and with absolute accuracy locate any form in the New Testament. We also suggest *Greek-English Analytical Concordance of the Greek-English New Testament* by John Stegenga.

In addition to lexicons, the student should have a number of sets of word studies. The reason why he should have more than one set is that often where one set of word studies does not offer any help on a word or a passage, another one will. Again, by using several word studies, the student can compare conflicting interpretations at times and thus come to a more intelligent and satisfying conclusion himself. We would like to mention two *musts* in word studies, two sets that will form companion studies which will supplement one another, both published by Wm. B. Eerdmans Publishing Co., of Grand Rapids, Michigan. They are *Expositor's Greek Testament* in five volumes, and *Vincent's Word Studies in the New Testament*, in four. While we cannot give a blanket endorsement of everything in these studies, yet on the whole they are generally sound. One could not hope for more in works that cover the whole field of Greek exegesis in the New Testament. The writer has used both for many years and has found them most helpful. Should the student desire other word studies, we would recommend *Alford's Greek Testament*. These are recommended for their accuracy and spiritual depth of interpretation.

The student needs a good Greek concordance. *Englishman's Greek Concordance of the New Testament* will give the Scripture location, the translation of the Greek word, and enough of the translation either before or after the word or both, so that one can recognize the context in which the word is found. The *Concordance of the Greek Testament* by W. F. Moulton and A. S. Geden is also a valuable lexicon to see where the word is used. If you would like a list of where the Greek word is used in the Septuagint (the Greek translation of the Old Testament) to gain insight into its use or illustrations of its use, try either *A Concordance of the Septuagint* by Hatch and Redpath or *A Concordance of the Septuagint* by George Morrish.

Two multiple volume sets are available which in themselves are a veritable library of information regarding Greek words. A three-volume set, *The New International Dictionary of New Testament Theology* edited by Colin Brown, is highly recommended for a study of the words in their secular (classical, papyri, church fathers, etc.) usage and their biblical (Septuagint and New Testament) usage. A ten-volume set, *Theological Dictionary of the New Testament* edited by Gerhard Kittel (translated by Geoffrey W. Bromiley) is similar to the former set, but more complete.

Finally, *Synonyms of the New Testament* by Archbishop Trench, is a most valuable work. This should prove a most enriching study, and a great help in the interpretation of the Greek New Testament.

Of course, the student should not work with an obsolete text. The texts by *Nestle,* or the one by the British and Foreign Bible Society (published in 1954) or *The Greek New Testament* (published by the United Bible Societies in 1966) are the best.

10

The Practical Method of Presenting the Added Light from the Greek Text

I T IS ONE thing to be able to work successfully in the Greek New Testament so as to bring out from the intricacies of its grammar and syntax, rich truth which is not brought over into the translations. It is quite another thing to be able to present that truth in a simple, pleasing, and effective way in the pulpit.

There are two things in this latter connection which must be avoided. One is *pedanticism*. There is no place in the Christian pulpit for a display or affectation of learning. Nor should there be any undue emphasis placed upon *minutiae* in the presentation of one's knowledge when preaching the Word. The trained exegete will leave the technicalities connected with the grammar and syntax of the Greek language, back where they belong, in his study. He will bring only the finished product with him into the pulpit. To talk about the aorist tense, for instance, to an audience that could not tell the difference between it and the side of a barn, is pedantic. To mention a Greek word in an address to an audience that does not know Greek, is likewise pedantic.

The other thing the expositor who uses his Greek New Testament, must be very careful to avoid, is that of *undermining the confidence of his audience in the standard, reliable translations*. It is the height of folly, when presenting some additional light from the Greek, to say, "Now, this is the way it is in the English translation, *but* this is the way it is in the Greek." That at once causes the audience to suspect that our translations are not correct. On the whole, our standard, reliable translations are correct. The corrections one might offer are few and far between. And those can be handled in another way.

The best approach is for the expositor to assure his audience that he is not offering any corrections upon the translation, but merely bringing out some details from the Greek text that cannot be brought over into a translation that is held down to a minimum of words. He should tell his hearers that the standard translations are the product of the combined skill of competent Greek scholars, and that, considering the difficulty of translating into English such a highly organized and specialized language as Greek, they are masterpieces of scholarship. He should inform them that the Greek language can concentrate more ideas in one word than the English can, and that the best the translators can do in a case like that, is to choose an English word that will give the reader the predominating idea in the Greek word, and leave such details as cannot be brought over into English, back in the Greek text. It is these details, these delicate shades of meaning, which the expositor is bringing out. He is a trained servant of God, chosen and equipped to bring to the saints, richer spiritual food, and a clearer understanding of the Word than they can obtain in the translations. The saints should therefore avail themselves of that ministry, either through the spoken or the written exposition of Scripture. Sinners on the whole have been saved by believing the translations, and saints have grown in grace by feeding on the same translations. But where a servant of God is equipped to bring out treasures from the Greek New Testament for the hungry saints, his ministry should be welcomed and taken advantage of.

We will now deal with the practical method of handling this added truth. Suppose the expositor is preaching in Romans 6, and he comes to the word "servants." He has made a thorough study of the Greek word there, and has read Deissmann's comment to the effect that the English word totally effaces the ancient significance of the Greek word. He will be tempted to use that statement as an effective background upon which to paint the richness of the Greek word. But upon reflection, he will come to the conclusion that while that procedure might be desirable from one standpoint, yet it would do more harm than good, since it would tend to undermine the confidence of his hearers in the English translation. Instead, he decides to handle the word as follows: "We come now to the study of the word 'servants.' The word which Paul uses here is a very rich word, full of meaning. Its secular usage, we shall see, brought over into the New Testament, is in exact accord with the doctrines of Christianity. Is it not wonderful that, in the providence of God, these Greek words which the Holy Spirit has caused the Bible writers to choose, were used in the secular world of the first century, in such a way that they would be fit instruments by which they could bring to us the truth which God desired us to have? The word means in the first place, 'one who is born into the condition and position of a slave.'" And then, the pastor proceeds to bring out the rich meaning of the Greek word without mentioning the word or causing the people to lose confidence in the reliability of their translations by showing the inadequacy in this instance, of the English word in rendering the Greek word.

If the pastor is not thoroughly trained in Greek, he, of course, does not want to give his people the impression that he is. He can adopt the following technique; "Greek scholars tell us that this word Paul uses is," and then proceed to tell his audience what they say about the word.

Suppose he is called upon to handle a place where, for instance, the King James Version contradicts itself, as in Philippians 3:12, 15, where Paul asserts that he was at that time not yet perfect, and yet includes himself among those who are perfect. The only right procedure is to tell his hearers that the English language is not equipped in the case of a translation which is held down to a minimum of words, to handle the intricate technicalities of the Greek in some instances. Then he should go on to show them that the Greek construction in verse 12 speaks of a completed process of sanctification and a condition of absolute spiritual maturity which Paul denies, and that the text of verse 15 refers to relative spiritual maturity. He should explain that this is no error on the part of the translators, but that the contradiction is due to the failure of the English to handle the Greek text here. He should assure them that such instances are few and far between.

Or, suppose that the pastor is giving a message on Ephesians 3:16-17, speaking on the vital relationship between the ministry of the Holy Spirit to the saint, and the indwelling of the Lord Jesus. The pastor is handling κατοικῆσαι, so full of meaning. He has taken the word apart and thoroughly analyzed it, and has come upon that rich nugget of truth, "That Christ may finally settle down and feel completely at home in your hearts." How will he handle that? Well, he will proceed as follows: "The word Paul uses is a wonderful word, full of rich meaning. The English word 'dwell' which our translators have given us, is an excellent rendering of it, for a one-word translation. It is a correct translation, and possibly the best word in all the English language to give the meaning of the Greek word. We want to study Paul's word for a little while tonight, and build the details that were left behind in the Greek text, around that word 'dwell.' The word has in it the idea of a home, and the making of one's home in a certain place. It also has the idea of the word 'down,' which suggests permanence. Thus, we have the idea of someone making his permanent home in a certain place. Indeed, this word was used of those who were permanent residents in a village, in contrast to those who were residing there only temporarily." And so the pastor goes on treating the word, much to the delight and edification of his hearers. He has not once mentioned the word, nor the tense involved, nor the prefixed preposition. But he has given the people enough so that they are assured that he is on solid ground in his exposition.

Well, what can he do with a statement like that of John the Baptist; "I indeed baptize you with water unto repentance" (Matt. 3:11)? The pastor knows very well that the word "unto" in this context, means "resulting in," as for example, "The gospel is the power of God unto (resulting in) salvation" (Rom. 1:16). He also knows that a mere ordinance is powerless to effect the person's repentance. He knows that this is one of the very few unfortunate translations in the King James Version. He is teaching the Gospel according to Matthew in his weekday Bible class. He could go about it in this way. "We want to study the word translated 'unto.' The same word is used by Matthew in chapter 12:41, where we have the words, 'The men of

Nineveh shall rise in judgment with this generation, and shall condemn it: because they repented at the preaching of Jonas.' The word 'at' is the translation of the same Greek word translated 'unto' in chapter 3:11. Now, Jonah did not preach because the Ninevites repented, but the Ninevites repented because of Jonah's preaching. Just so, the converts of John the Baptist did not repent because he baptized them, but he baptized them because they repented. Therefore, the idea here is that John baptized them because of their repentance."

Whether the pastor will say that the word "unto" here leaves the wrong impression with the English reader, will depend upon circumstances. If his class has confidence in him as a Bible expositor, and is made up of informed Christians, he may tell them plainly that it is an erroneous translation of the Greek word in this context. Or, if someone insists that this verse teaches baptismal regeneration, it is time for the pastor to label things in a positive way. But in general, the less that is said about a certain translation that is not up to par, the better. But silence at the expense of truth is not the proper procedure either.

A distinction should be made between the handling of the Greek text in the pulpit on the Lord's Day morning with a large audience in the church, and its presentation in a Bible class. In the former case, technicalities and detail should be left out. One cannot afford to spend too much time on single words. But in a Bible class, the expositor can emphasize word studies, and even go into technicalities and dwell on detail. But the Greek text should enrich every message the pastor gives. The above method of handling the extra light from the Greek, need be used only where the interpretation departs noticeably from the translation, or consists of much added material. As a general rule, the expositor can bring out the material from the Greek text and the clearer light which it affords, without mentioning the Greek at all.

The pastor should not be at all hesitant about using his Greek in the pulpit. When his people know that he is a diligent student of the Word, and spends his time in intensive study in his preparation for his messages instead of sipping pink tea with the ladies, when they know that he brings the tools of Greek scholarship to the study of the Word, they will think all the more of him for it. There is no premium put upon ignorance. An educated ministry that is spiritual, is one of the most beautiful things in all the world. A pastor, trained to his finger-tips, filled with the Holy Spirit, presents the ideal combination for effective service.

11

The Practical Place of the Holy Spirit in the Interpretation of the Greek New Testament

I N THE introduction to his translation of the Greek New Testament, a present day scholar, when commenting upon the difficulties attendant upon the translation of that portion of the Bible, says; "But once the translator of the New Testament is freed from the influence of the theory of verbal inspiration, these difficulties cease to be so formidable." The fact that this translator does not believe in the verbal inspiration of the original texts, allows him a certain unjustified freedom in his translation work. As a case in point, take his translation in Romans 1:16; "I am proud of the gospel," where the King James Version has, "I am not ashamed of the gospel." But αἰσχύνομαι means "to be ashamed," and even though it is negated by οὐ, it does not mean, "I am proud." Verbal inspiration demands that the translator hold to the exact meaning of the word in the original, and not offer an interpretation of his own, based upon the general idea which he may think he finds in the sentence.

The first question which the expositor must settle for himself is therefore, as to just how close he will keep to the *words* of the Greek text. If he believes in verbal inspiration, he will hold himself to an exact translation of every *word*. He will give every *word* its full force. He will see that the weight of his translation will be supported by every *word*. He will bring the weight of his exegesis to bear down heavily on every *word*.

The Bible writers claim verbal inspiration for themselves. By verbal inspiration we mean that each word in the original Hebrew and Greek manuscripts, was chosen out of the vocabulary of the writer by the Holy Spirit. Those words were chosen whose content of meaning was such that they would exactly represent the truth which God wished the human race to have. Peter describes this process in his second epistle (1:21). The Greek here is, "Through the personal agency of the Holy Spirit being brought forward in speech, men spoke from God." The word "moved" is the translation of φέρω which has the meaning in the passive voice of "being brought forward in speech." "By" is the translation of ὑπό, the preposition of personal agency. The word ἁγίου occurs with πνεύματος in the text and is in the genitive case, showing that it modifies the word "Spirit," not "men." ἀπὸ θεοῦ is ablative of source, and modifies the verb "spoke." These men spoke from God as a source. That means that their speaking found its source in God. Speaking implies the use of words. That means that the words these men spoke were given them by God.

Paul in 1 Corinthians 2:13 also claims verbal inspiration for the manuscripts of the Bible. He speaks in verse 10 of the act of God the Holy Spirit imparting to the Bible writers, truth incapable of being discovered by man's unaided reason. This impartation is described by the word

ἀποκαλύπτω which refers to the act of uncovering something that was previously hidden from view. Then he
describes the process by which the writers wrote down
that truth, in the word συνκρίνω. He asserts that the Bible
writers spoke, that is, put in words the truth revealed, not
by choosing words which *their* learning led them to select,
but which the Holy Spirit caused them to choose.

But the process was not one of a mechanical dictation of
words by the Holy Spirit. The Bible writers were allowed
the free play of their personalities, their mental processes,
and their learning, under the guidance of the Holy Spirit.
The word συνκρίνω means literally, "to judge with," that
is, "to judge something with something else so as to match
the two things." Thayer gives, "to join together fitly."
The Bible writers, with the truth in their minds, searched
their Greek vocabularies for the exact Greek word which
in each case would adequately convey the truth which God
gave them. They, led by the Holy Spirit, would compare
the particular truth with a certain word, discard that word
for another, until they were assured by the Spirit that they
had chosen the correct word. Thus the process went on.
They matched Spirit-taught words with spiritual truth.

Well, of what value is all this to an expositor who
believes the Bible's claim for itself as to the verbal inspiration of its original manuscripts? He will treat every *word*
in the original text. He will put the proper value on every
word. He will not skim over the surface and give his
general interpretation of the sentence in question, but will
allow each *word* to take him where it wills in the truth.
He will translate and interpret faithfully, even though some
of the truth brought out, he will not understand at first,
perhaps never. He will be an *exegete*, taking out of the text
that which is there, not an *eisegete*, injecting into the text
that which is not there.

Verbal inspiration extends to the choice of synonyms. This fact will help one, for instance, in the problem of the use of the words ἀγαπάω and φιλέω in our Lord's conversation with Peter (John 21:15-18). The argument is put forth that because this conversation was not in Greek but rather in Aramaic, the two words for love here are not to be distinguished in meaning. *If one believes in verbal inspiration, that argument is entirely beside the point.* John, when about to write the account of this conversation, had that conversation in mind in the Aramaic words which were used, and for two reasons; first, because he remembered it in the words that were used, and second, because, being a Jew, his mental processes would be in his mother tongue. But, when he was about to write the account in Greek, he would be forced to search his Greek vocabulary for the exact Greek words which would adequately express the words of the Lord Jesus to Peter, and Peter's words to Him. Here is where the ministry of the Spirit came in, and verbal inspiration. The words ἀγαπάω and φιλέω had by this time (A.D. 90-95), a fixed content of meaning by reason of their use in previous New Testament books, ἀγαπάω in 1 Corinthians 13, John 3:16; Romans 5:5; Galatians 5:22, and φιλέω in such scriptures as Matthew 6:5; 23:6; 26:48; Luke 20:46. John, thus guided by the Spirit, chose the right synonym in each case that would express exactly what Jesus meant and what Peter meant. All the New Testament writers with the exception of Luke, were Jews, and therefore thought in Aramaic. When writing the New Testament, they had to take the truth which they had in their mother tongue, and put it into Greek. Verbal inspiration guarantees the exact translation into Greek, of ideas which were held by the writer in another language.

Verbal inspiration extends not only to the choice of words, but also to the tense, mood, and voice of verbs, the gender, number, and case of nouns, to all grammatical and syntactical technicalities in the original text, for words are understood in their grammatical forms and syntactical relationships. The Greek of the New Testament is the same as the international, *Koine* Greek of the Roman world. It was the Greek spoken in ordinary conversation by those who used it as their second language. The writers wrote to be understood. If they expected to be clearly and accurately understood, they had to follow the grammar and syntax of the Greek of the first century world. The Holy Spirit saw to it that they did. How else can one account for the wonderful and delicate distinctions in the Greek text, in the case of such writers as Peter and John, who did not have the training in Greek that Luke and Paul had? Thus, the expositor cannot only bear down heavily on the exact meaning of words, but also on the technicalities of grammar and syntax. These provide just as sure a foundation as Greek words. And because of that, 'interpretation of the Greek text which adheres closely to the tried and proved rules of Greek grammar and syntax, becomes almost as exact a science as that of mathematics. Take, for instance, the rule which says that the word in the accusative case is closely associated with the verbal form in the sentence. That settles beyond the peradventure of a doubt, the meaning of Jude 6-7, and the controversy as to whether the angels committed fornication. Or, take the rule that a pronoun must agree with its antecedent in gender. That settles the question in Romans 6:12, as to whether Paul refers to the lusts of sin or of the body. *There is no appeal from decisions that are based on such universally acknowledged rules of syntax as these.* Thus, when an expositor relies upon the verbal inspiration of the Greek text, he knows where he is. But, should he deviate in the least from this doctrine, he is all at sea, and the Greek text, instead of being an objective revelation to him, becomes a subjective problem, and is at the mercy of every whim of contemporary standards that are as relative and fluid as the theories of men and the changing ethics of the philosopher. The first place which the Holy Spirit occupies, therefore, in the interpretation of the Greek text, is in His work of verbal inspiration.

Now, after having brought about an infallible transmission of the truth from the heart of God to the written manuscripts, the Holy Spirit stands ready to be the interpreter of that which He has caused to be written down. This is His present ministry for the expositor of the Greek New Testament.

To the expositor who loves his Greek New Testament, that book is one of the most beautiful things in the world. There he sits at his study table, his Greek New Testament under the desk lamp which sheds its glow over its sacred page. The letters themselves are beautiful. There are all the intricacies of tense, mood, and voice, gender, number and case. There are the prepositions and particles, the participles and infinitives, the conjunctions and articles, with a meaning all their own for the one who has eyes to see, Greek eyes. Every word is alive with divine life because chosen by the Holy Spirit and energized with divine fire from the altars of heaven itself. There it lies, the Greek New Testament, vibrant with life and with the message it is eager to impart. The expositor, let us say, has been trained in the grammar and syntax of New Testament Greek. At his disposal are a row of lexicons, shelves of word studies, and other Greek tools. But all this is of little avail unless he has an intelligent understanding of and

correct adjustment to the Holy Spirit in His personal
ministry to his life and his understanding and exposition
of the Word.

The great apostle, himself an accomplished scholar in
the Greek classics and in Greek philosophy, writing to the
Greeks at Corinth says, "The natural man receiveth not
the things of the Spirit of God: for they are foolishness
unto him: neither can he know them, because they are
spiritually discerned" (1 Cor. 2:14). The word "natural" is
the translation of ψυχικός. This word was coined by
Aristotle to distinguish the pleasures of the soul, such as
ambition and desire for knowledge, from those of the
body. Polybius and Plutarch say that "Contrasted with the
ἀκρατής (the powerless man, the man who is without
power or command over himself or his passions), the
ψυχικός is the noblest of men." This word therefore
describes to the Corinthian Greeks, the unregenerate man
at his best, the man commended by philosophy, the man
who is actuated by the higher thoughts and aims of the
natural life.

When Paul uses this term, he is not speaking of the
average unsaved man, nor of unsaved humanity as a
whole, but of the unsaved Greek who is educated to his
finger tips, the man who is skilled in Greek philosophy
and rhetoric, and who has a well-trained and a keen mind.
It is true that no unsaved person is equipped to understand
the deep things of God's Word. But Paul is emphasizing
the fact here that even highly trained scholars are just as
helpless as any other unsaved person to understand it.
Scholarship, devoid of the Holy Spirit, is unable to work
successfully in the Greek New Testament. Paul, therefore,
contrasts the man whose understanding of the truth depends solely upon natural insight, the ψυχικός man, with
the man whose understanding of the truth depends upon

his reliance upon the Holy Spirit, the πνευματικός man, saying that the Word of God is understood by means of the illumination afforded by the Spirit.

No natural light in itself and by itself ever disclosed the depths of meaning in the Greek New Testament to the expositor. His brilliant intellect, highly-trained mind, mental acumen, his expert grasp of the rules of Greek grammar and syntax, all these are in themselves, mere natural light. The expositor whose only reliance is upon these, is working in the dark.

But with the light cast upon the sacred page of the Greek New Testament which the Holy Spirit affords, all is different. Then the Greek words, tenses, moods, and voices, the genders, numbers, and cases, the synonyms, prepositions, articles, participles, infinitives, adverbs, adjectives, all spring to life, and the expositor is confronted with so much truth, so many different and delicate shades of meaning, that he is at a loss where to start first in tabulating and assimilating such fabulous wealth. What was in itself mere natural light, now becomes the very means which the Holy Spirit uses to bring to the expositor, riches from the gold mine of truth in the Greek New Testament.

John in his first epistle (2:20, 27), speaks of this teaching ministry of the Holy Spirit in which He, the divine author of the Greek New Testament, interprets its meaning to the Christian expositor. He says, "Ye have an unction from the Holy One, and ye know all things." The word "unction" is the translation of χρῖσμα, allied to χρίω, the word in the New Testament which is used exclusively for the anointing with the Holy Spirit, ἀλείφω being used of the anointing with oil. The unction therefore to which John refers here is the anointing with the Spirit. This anointing, he says, results in the believer knowing all

things. The words, "ye know all things" are a translation
based upon a reading that has been rejected by Nestle, this
textual critic believing that the original text of John,
instead of having πάντα, the neuter accusative plural, had
πάντες, masculine nominative plural. The translation
reads, "All ye, know." That is, because all believers have
the anointing with the Spirit, therefore, all believers know.
John is speaking in this context of the believer in his
relation to the various false teachers who exhibit the spirit
of antichrist. These latter do not have the Holy Spirit, nor
do their teachings show that they have the ability to know
the truth as it is in Christ Jesus. But, because believers
have the anointing with the Spirit, they have the ability to
know the truth. The word "know" here is the translation
of οἶδα, which means "to know, to understand, to per-
ceive." That is, the ability to understand the Word of God
is a spiritual possession of the believer by virtue of the fact
that he is anointed with the Spirit. In verse 27 we have the
statement that this anointing teaches the saint, so that he
understands the Word. But this anointing is the Holy
Spirit Himself who indwells the believer. The anointing
with the Spirit refers to the act of God the Father causing
the Holy Spirit to take up His permanent residence in the
heart of the saint in answer to the prayer of God the Son.[1]
This takes place just once, when the believing sinner
places his faith in the Lord Jesus as his Savior. There is no
fresh anointing, for there is no repeated coming of the
Spirit into the heart of the believer.

But now, we must make a careful distinction. While the
anointing with the Spirit makes possible His teaching
ministry to the saint, it does not determine the fulness,
richness, efficiency, or extent of that ministry. Every saint
is anointed with the Spirit. But every saint is not the
recipient of the best services of the Spirit in His teaching

ministry. That which determines the clearness and depth of understanding of the Word on the part of the expositor, is the degree to which he is controlled by the Holy Spirit. And that which determines the latter, is his degree of yieldedness to the Spirit. In other words, while the Spirit's ministry of causing the expositor to understand the meaning of the Greek New Testament, is potential in His indwelling of the saint, His teaching ministry is operative only to the extent that the saint is filled with Him, or in other words, controlled by Him. The anointing of itself does not result in the teaching. It is as the expositor is filled with the Spirit, that His ministry of teaching is performed. Of course, the Spirit does the best He can in teaching a saint who is not wholly yielded. But as in the case of a student who does not want to be taught, the teacher can make little headway, so in the case of the saint who lives an unyielded life, the great Teacher can do but little teaching.

The important point therefore is, that there is a vital connection between the expositor's understanding of the Word, and his personal holiness of life and yieldedness to the Holy Spirit. When the Holy Spirit finds an expositor who has been trained in Greek, and who is willing to do exhaustive, hard, laborious, and painstaking study in the Greek New Testament, when He finds that that expositor is living a life of personal holiness and separation, a life fully yielded, and that the expositor desires a deep and thorough knowledge of the Greek New Testament in order that the Lord Jesus might be glorified in his exposition of the Word, then things happen. The expositor marvels at the clearness with which he now understands the Word. He is lost in wonder at the depth and richness of meaning that are his as he studies his Greek text. He is delighted at the ease with which he now solves exegetical problems that before were mysteries to him. He finds great satisfaction in the new power that is his when he teaches and preaches the Word, in the new confidence he has as he gives it out, and in the freshness and originality which his presentation possesses.

The practical place of the Holy Spirit in the interpretation of the Greek New Testament is therefore two-fold. The first has to do with the verbal inspiration of the Greek text. When an expositor works on that principle, he pays attention to each word and grammatical form and syntactical relation. He translates and interprets the text faithfully. The second has to do with His teaching ministry. When the expositor is living a yielded, Spirit-filled life, and recognizes the Spirit as his Teacher, and depends upon Him for that ministry, he becomes the recipient of the Spirit's work of causing him to understand the meaning of the Greek New Testament.

The great Greek scholar, James Hope Moulton, beautifully expresses the above truth in his poem, "At The Classroom Door."

Lord, at Thy word opens yon door, inviting
  Teacher and taught to feast this hour with Thee;
Opens a Book where God in human writing
  Thinks His deep thoughts, and dead tongues live for me.
Too dread the task, too great the duty calling,
  Too heavy far the weight is laid on me!
O if mine own thought should on Thy words falling
  Mar the great message, and men hear not Thee!
Give me Thy voice to speak, Thine ear to listen,
  Give me Thy mind to grasp Thy mystery;

So shall my heart throb, and my glad eyes glisten,
Rapt with the wonders Thou dost show to me.

---

1. For a study of the anointing with, the baptism by, and the fulness of the
Spirit see *Untranslatable Riches*, Wuest, pp. 74-103.

SCRIPTURE INDEX

Matthew

1:16 28
2:13 68
3:6 101-102
3:7 . . . . .100, 102
3:10-12 73
3:11 . . . .30, 59-60, 100-101, 139-140
3:16 100
4:4 47
5:8 81
6:5 146
7:4 102
7:7 55
10:8 33
11:1 102
11:3 72
11:13-14 102
11:16 102
12:32 80
12:41 . . . . .60, 139
15:2 102
17:2 86
20:22-23 102
21:25 102
23:6 146
23:37, 39 73
26:39 58
26:48 146
28:19 102

Mark

1:4-5, 8-9 102
1:8 100
2:9 54
7:4 100
7:8 102
9:22 24
10:38-39 . . . . .99, 102
11:30 102
14:71 93

Luke

2:1 80
3:3 102
3:7 100
3:7, 12, 16, 21 102
7:29-30 102
11:11 58
11:38 . . . . .100, 102
12:50 102
16:24 99-100
18:22 55
20:4 102
20:46 146

John

1:1 . . . . 16, 67
1:3 66
1:11 68
1:12 . . . . 51, 54
1:25, 26, 28, 31, 33 102
1:31, 33 75
1:33 100
3:7 36
3:16 146
3:22-25 101
3:22-23, 26 102
4:1-2 102
4:11 17
4:13-14 43
4:24 19
5:20 78
5:40 68
6:19 69
10:17-18 61
10:27-30 50
10:40 102
13:6-10 75
13:26 100
15:7 . . . . .50, 107
16:14 40

16:27 78
19:30 49
21:3 45
21:8 31
21:18 77
21:15-18 146

Acts

1:5 . . . . 100, 102
1:22 102
2:23 22
2:38 60
2:38, 41 102
6:1-6 125
8:12-13, 16, 36, 38 102
9:18 102
10:37 102
10:47-48 102
11:16 . . . . 100, 102
11:18 59
13:9 119
13:24 102
16:15, 33 102
16:30-31 . . . . 52, 54
17:6 80
17:24 80
18:8 102
18:25 102
19:3-4 102
19:4-5 101-102
20:28 124
20:35 81
21:37 52
22:3 67
22:16 . . . . 100, 102

Romans

1:16 . . . . 59, 139, 143
1:21 94
5:5 146
5:20 68
5:21 21
6 . . . . 102, 137
6:1 . . . . 21, 45
6:2-14 45
6:3-4 . . . . 32, 97-98, 103
6:12 . . . . .27, 147
6:13 50
6:15 45
6:16-17 88
8:20 94
8:30 48
12:2 . . . . 43, 87

1 Corinthians

1:13-17 102
1:14 100
2:10, 13 144
2:14 149
10:2 103
12:13 . . . . 32, 100, 105
13 . . . . .78, 146
15:29 102
11:13-15 86

Galatians

1:4 80
1:6-7 73
1:8-9 93
1:16 94
3:6 17
3:23 17
3:26 18
3:27 100
4:19 39
5:22 146
6:1 91
6:11-18 41

Ephesians

1:3 81
2:8 48
3:9-10 66
3:14-21 90
3:16 138
3:17 . . . . .60, 138
4:5 100
4:11 23
4:12-13 76
5:11 43
5:25 78

Philippians

1:3-5 . . . . 24, 63
2:5-8 57
2:6-7 . . . . 83, 85
3:12, 15 . . . . .46, 138
3:13 65
4:6 43

Colossians

2:12 100

Thessalonians

4:13-18 95

1 Timothy

3:2, 12 21
3 125

2 Timothy

4:7 51

Titus

3:5 103

Hebrews

1:6 81
2:5 80
5:7 63-65
5:8 18
6:2 102
6:13 93
9:10 . . . . .99, 101-102
10:9 58
10:12 49
10:22-23 101
12:2 . . . . 57-58, 64

James

4:5 61

1 Peter

1:7 28
1:18 94
3:1 19
3:3 80
3:18-25 112
3:21 102
5:9 112
5:10 65

2 Peter

1:1 23
1:21 144

1 John

2:15 . . . . 44, 80
2:20, 27 150
3:4 19
3:9 44
4:8 18-19

Jude

6-7 . . . . 32, 147

Revelation

5:10 69
7:14 20
19:13 100